DEAN CHRISTOPHER

Minimalism

A 12-Week Guide to Decluttering Life for Peace, Clarity and Purpose

Copyright © 2023 by Dean Christopher

All rights reserved. No part of this publication may be reproduced, stored or transmitted in any form or by any means, electronic, mechanical, photocopying, recording, scanning, or otherwise without written permission from the publisher. It is illegal to copy this book, post it to a website, or distribute it by any other means without permission.

First edition

*This book was professionally typeset on Reedsy.
Find out more at reedsy.com*

Contents

Why Minimalism?	1
Understanding The Minimalist Lifestyle	4
Minimalist Mindset - Finding Joy in Simple Pleasures	11
Understanding Habit Stacking	15
Week 1: Creating a Minimalist Living Space	20
Week 2: Simple Scheduling & Prioritising	49
Week 3: Cultivating Gratitude and Finding Happiness	62
Week 4: Minimalise Mind Clutter	65
Week 5: Digital Detox - Downsizing Your Technology	80
Week 6: Simplifying Your Diet & Nutrition	92
Week 7: Creating a Minimalist Budget	116
Week 8: Finding Work-Life Balance	129
Week 9: Embracing Slow Living	157
Week 10: Crafting A Minimalist Exercise Routine	179
Week 11: Simplifying Relationships for Deeper Connections	202
Week 12: Living Sustainably Through Minimalism	212
Conclusion: Your New Mindful Habits for Peace and Clarity	223
Thank You for Reading Mindful Minimalism	227

Why Minimalism?

Life can be overwhelming, and striking a balance between work, personal commitments, and leisure can be challenging, to say the least.

As we navigate the complexities of modern life, we may find ourselves feeling stressed, anxious, and unfulfilled.

This is where minimalism comes in.

As I reflect on my own journey towards minimalism, I realise that it has been a brilliant way to find balance in my once too busy life.

Like many of us, I often felt overwhelmed by the sheer number of tasks and obligations that demanded my attention. As someone who tends to be over-ambitious, I struggled with wanting to do everything, only to end up feeling burnt out and unproductive.

I know first-hand that there is only so much time in a day, and it can be challenging to balance all of life's responsibilities while still finding time to enjoy the ride. I've also learned, through practice, that a minimalist approach to life can help even those with the busiest lives and that physical clutter also manifests emotional clutter.

Slowing down and simplifying my life through minimalism has helped me to gain more time and to truly savour each moment, rather than feeling like time is slipping away quickly.

By simplifying our surroundings, schedules, and priorities, we can focus our energy on what truly matters and let go of the rest.

So if you're feeling overwhelmed and struggling to find balance, know that you're not alone and that minimalism might just be the solution you've been seeking.

Incorporating minimalism into our lives can provide a framework for simplifying and streamlining our daily routines.

Even for busy individuals, minimalism can help to reduce stress, increase productivity, and allow for more time to focus on the things that bring joy and fulfilment.

By reducing the clutter in your physical environment and simplifying your schedule, you will be able to create more time and space for the things that bring you joy and fulfilment.

In addition, minimalism encourages a more intentional and mindful approach to life, which can help busy individuals feel a better sense of clarity, peace of mind, and overall confidence.

By being more selective about what we allow into our lives, we can make better choices about how we spend our time and energy. This can lead to a greater sense of purpose and fulfilment, even in the midst of a busy and demanding schedule.

Ultimately, minimalism can help busy individuals create a more balanced and fulfilling life that aligns with our true priorities and values.

Understanding The Minimalist Lifestyle

Living a minimalist lifestyle is not just about decluttering your space and getting rid of excess belongings.

It is a journey towards finding peace and meaning in life through the pursuit of simplicity.

This can be a daunting task for many, as the journey towards minimalism can be stressful and overwhelming. Decluttering a cluttered life, space, and mind is not a quick or easy task!

However, you don't have to do it all at once. You also don't need to do it all in 12 weeks!

If there's one thing I've learned that's helped me the most it's to *'not be so hard on yourself'*.

This book is a starter guide to living out your life the minimalist way (and doing it your way).

It is possible to embark on this journey with low stress and ease, using the 12-week guide provided in this book & a slow-living mindset.

The minimalist movement has been around for centuries, with teachings that can be traced back to ancient philosophers and spiritual leaders. The Buddha encouraged detachment from material possessions and the pursuit of a simple life.

Detachment from material possessions can have numerous benefits, including:

- Reduced stress:

Owning too many possessions can be overwhelming and stressful. Detachment from material possessions can help reduce stress levels and create a more peaceful living environment.

- Increased clarity and focus:

When you're not constantly surrounded by material possessions, it can be easier to focus on the things that matter most in life. This can help bring clarity to your thoughts and actions.

- Improved financial situation:

By detaching from material possessions, you may be able to save money and improve your financial situation. You may be less likely to make impulse purchases or accumulate debt.

- More meaningful relationships:

When you're not focused on material possessions, you may be more present and engaged in your relationships. This can lead to deeper and more meaningful connections with others.

- Environmental benefits:

Owning and consuming fewer material possessions can have a positive impact on the environment. It can reduce waste, lower your consumption, and promote sustainable living.

- Improved confidence and self-esteem:

Focusing on internal values rather than material possessions helps you recognise what you already possess within. If you know you are kind and true then nothing you can own will take away from your inherent goodness as a person. By letting go of the need to constantly accumulate things, individuals can gain a sense of self-worth and purpose beyond material goods.

In the modern era, influential figures have advocated for a less-is-more approach to lifestyle design, and minimalism has gained popularity around the world as people seek to escape the trappings of consumerism and find more purpose and joy in their lives.

To live a minimalist lifestyle, one must first understand what minimalism truly means.

It is not just about owning fewer possessions or living in a smaller home. It is a mindset that encourages intentionality, mindfulness, and clarity. It is about creating space in your life for the things that truly matter, whether that be relationships, experiences, or personal growth.

By eliminating distractions and focusing on what truly brings us joy and meaning, we can live more fulfilled and purposeful lives.

However, the road to minimalism can be challenging, especially in a society that values material possessions and consumerism.

It can be hard to let go of things we've accumulated over the years, whether they hold sentimental value or not. It can also be difficult to break the habit of constantly acquiring new things.

The good news is that you don't have to do it alone. The 12-week guide provided in this book offers a comprehensive roadmap for those seeking to simplify their lives and find greater peace and meaning.

The guide is designed to be a gradual and manageable process. Each week focuses on a different aspect of minimalism, from decluttering and organising your physical space to cultivating mindfulness and intentionality in your daily habits.

The guide is flexible, allowing readers to adapt the steps to their own pace and lifestyle.

It encourages readers to start small and build on their progress each week, rather than trying to make drastic changes all at once.

The first week of the guide focuses on starting the process of decluttering and simplifying your physical space. This is an essential step in the journey towards minimalism, as physical clutter can create mental clutter and stress.

By letting go of possessions that no longer serve a purpose or bring us joy, we can create more space and clarity in our homes and minds. The guide provides practical tips for decluttering and organising each area of the home, from the kitchen to the closet.

As readers progress through the guide, they will begin to focus on cultivating mindfulness and intentionality in their daily habits.

This includes things like practising gratitude, setting intentions, and developing a regular meditation practice. Throughout this book, you will discover the mindful practices that work best for you.

As a minimalist, you don't need to take all of them into your daily life, try them out and stick with the practices and habits that you feel serve you best.

By slowing down and being more present in our daily lives, we can begin to appreciate the simple joys and pleasures that are often overlooked in our fast-paced world.

Living a minimalist lifestyle is not about deprivation or sacrifice. It's about finding joy and meaning in the things that truly matter.

It's about creating space in our lives for the things that bring us fulfilment, whether that be spending time with loved ones, pursuing our passions, or simply enjoying a quiet moment of reflection.

The 12-week guide provided in this book offers a practical and manageable roadmap for those seeking to simplify their lives and find greater peace and meaning.

Living a minimalist lifestyle is not about becoming a master of minimalism in just 12 weeks.

It's about adopting a mindset of simplicity, intentionality, and mindfulness that gradually becomes a way of life.

The 12-week guide provided in this book is not meant to be overwhelming or a source of pressure, but rather a tool to help break down the journey towards minimalism into simple and achievable tasks.

By introducing one easy habit per week and slowly building on these habits. You will be better equipped to live a more simple, peaceful, and minimalist lifestyle after the 12-week period.

It's important to note that there's no such thing as a "master of minimalism." Instead, it's a continuous journey towards greater clarity, purpose, and joy in life. The key is to start small, be patient with oneself, and gradually integrate minimalism into every aspect of life.

After reading this book and going through the 12 weeks you will understand how to do that and the knowledge and experience you gain will stay with you for life.

So let us begin this journey with an open heart and a willingness to let go of what no longer serves us.

Let us create space in our lives for what truly matters and embrace the peace and fulfilment that comes with living a minimalist lifestyle.

Minimalist Mindset - Finding Joy in Simple Pleasures

In our modern world, it's easy to get caught up in the endless pursuit of more.

We're bombarded with messages that tell us we need the latest and greatest gadgets, the trendiest clothes, and the most luxurious homes.

It's easy to believe that these things will bring us happiness, but the truth is that they often leave us feeling unfulfilled.

The minimalist mindset is about learning to find joy in simple pleasures.

It's about recognising that happiness doesn't come from material possessions but from within.

When we shift our focus from what we don't have to what we do have, we begin to see the beauty and wonder in the world around us.

One of the simplest ways to cultivate a minimalist mindset is to start by appreciating the simple things in life.

This could be something as small as a cup of coffee in the morning or a walk in the park.

When we learn to find joy in the little things, we begin to realize that we don't need much to be truly happy.

When we cultivate a sense of gratitude for what we have, we begin to realise that we already have everything we need to be happy.

Gratitude is a powerful practice that can transform our lives. When we focus on what we're grateful for, we begin to see the abundance in our lives. We begin to feel more content and less anxious about what we don't have.

Finally, the minimalist mindset is about living intentionally. It's about being mindful of our actions and the impact they have on our lives and the lives of others.

When we live intentionally, we begin to make choices that align with our values and bring us closer to the life we want to live.

Living intentionally means making conscious choices about how we spend our time, what we bring into our lives, and how we interact with the world around us. It means being present in the moment and making the most of every experience.

Adopting a minimalist mindset can help to reduce stress in life. When you simplify your life, you eliminate many of the distractions and pressures that can cause anxiety and tension. By focusing on what truly matters and letting go of the unnecessary, you create a sense of calm and clarity in your mind.

In a minimalist mindset, you learn to appreciate the small things in life and find joy in simple pleasures.

You might take a walk in nature and enjoy the beauty of the trees and the birds singing. Or you might savour a cup of tea or coffee, enjoying the aroma and the taste without the need for any additional distractions.

By taking the time to appreciate these simple pleasures, you can reduce stress and anxiety, and create a sense of peace and contentment in your life.

This mindset helps you to stay in the present moment, rather than constantly worrying about the future or dwelling on the past.

It allows you to appreciate the beauty and wonder of life as it unfolds before you, rather than being caught up in the distractions and stressors of daily life.

In essence, a minimalist mindset encourages you to slow down and enjoy life's simple pleasures. It helps you to recognise that you don't need to constantly strive for more in order to find happiness and contentment.

When reading this book I would highly encourage you to

adopt this minimalist mindset as you embark on the 12-week program.

In conclusion, the minimalist mindset is about finding joy in simple pleasures, letting go of our attachment to material possessions, cultivating gratitude, and living intentionally.

When we embrace these principles, we begin to see that happiness doesn't come from what we own externally but from how we perceive life from within.

We begin to find joy in the little things and appreciate the beauty of the world around us.

Understanding Habit Stacking

Congratulations on starting this 12-week journey towards a minimalist lifestyle.

We have talked about the importance of cultivating a minimalist mindset and finding joy in simple pleasures. Now it's time to take action and make some changes in our daily routines.

But making significant changes in our lives can be challenging, especially when we try to do too much at once.

That's where habit stacking comes in. Habit stacking is a simple yet effective technique that can help us introduce new habits into our daily routines without overwhelming ourselves.

The idea behind habit stacking is to add one new habit at a time and then keep it up throughout the 12 weeks. By the end of the program, you'll have 12 new habits that you'll be incorporating into your life to help you live a more minimalist lifestyle.

Here's how it works: each week, you'll be adding one new habit to your daily routine. The habits will start simple, and each week we'll be building upon the previous habits until we have created a solid foundation for a more minimalist lifestyle.

For example, in the first week, we'll be focusing on something simple like decluttering one area of our home for 15 minutes each day. In week two, we'll be adding another more simple habit such as practising gratitude each day.

By week 12, you'll have 12 new habits that you'll be incorporating into your daily routine, and you'll be amazed at how much progress you've made.

Habit stacking is an effective way to build new habits and make lasting changes in our lives. By adding one new habit per week, we can create a foundation for a more minimalist lifestyle that is sustainable and manageable.

So, let's get started and see where this 12-week journey takes us.

It's important to note that while the 12-week program is designed in a specific order, you can feel free to adjust it to fit your personal needs. For example, if you're struggling with financial issues, you may want to prioritise the budgeting chapter and make that your first week.

The goal is to introduce one new habit per week and slowly build on that habit by "stacking" additional habits on top of it.

By the end of the 12 weeks, you'll have 12 new habits that you can incorporate into your daily routine to help you live a more minimalist and intentional life. So feel free to adjust the order of the chapters as needed to make the program work best for you.

Many people tend to associate minimalism purely with decluttering, but it encompasses so much more than that. In fact, it involves a complete shift in mindset and philosophy towards intentional living and finding joy in everyday moments.

As you embark on this 12-week journey, you will come to realise that minimalism is not just about getting rid of material possessions, but about living with a purpose and embracing a simpler way of life.

Unlike other programs that may focus on decluttering specific areas of your home week by week, this program takes a holistic approach to decluttering your entire life.

Starting from week 1, you will make a plan to gradually declutter your outer space by the end of week 12 and to keep your space clutter-free beyond this program.

Additionally, from then on, each week you will learn and adopt small habits to go alongside your decluttering plan that will greatly benefit you on your minimalist journey.

Decluttering both your outer living space and your inner head space.

You may also want to go through the program more than once to really enforce these habits.

If you ever feel overwhelmed in life further down the line because you've let some things slip, just remember, don't be hard on yourself and you can always come back and start this simple program again if needed.

By the end of the 12 week program, you will:

- Have created a tidy and clutter-free living space
- Incorporate the right daily habits to keep tidy and clean
- Have a calmer mind and sense of clarity
- Manage stressful situations better
- Feel more gratitude and positivity
- Have more time for things that bring you joy and fulfilment
- Feel a newfound sense of purpose

As you embark on this minimalist journey, you might find that certain chapters, like 'Simplifying Your Diet,' tackle complex subjects.

Don't be overwhelmed by the wealth of information in these larger chapters – it's all designed to help you step into a simpler, more intentional way of living.

The true essence of minimalist living unfolds in the action steps at the end of each chapter.

By following these steps, you will begin to cultivate positive minimalist habits in a straightforward and accessible manner.

If you ever need to revisit a particular concept or detail to help with your action tasks, you can always return to the reference point you need from earlier in the chapter.

Week 1: Creating a Minimalist Living Space

Note: You will notice this chapter is a lot larger than the others but don't worry! This is because this week we will start our main task of decluttering, but we won't be aiming to finish this all in one week. Remember this is a weekly habit staking program!

You can skim through the headers in this chapter and skip to the end where you will see your action steps for the week and how you will incorporate the decluttering process throughout the 12-week program.

The action steps relate back to what is written in this chapter and can be referred back to throughout the course of the program.

****

Welcome to Week 1 of our minimalist lifestyle program!

This week, we will be focusing on creating space in our homes by decluttering and adopting a minimalist approach to our living spaces.

The physical environment that surrounds us has a significant impact on our mental and emotional states.

Therefore, creating a simple, clutter-free environment can help us feel more peaceful, clear-headed, and focused.

In this chapter, we'll explore how to start decluttering and creating a minimalist home, with a focus on responsible disposal of items and creating space in our wardrobes, kitchens, bathrooms, and the rest of our living spaces.

Creating a minimalist home is one of the essential steps towards a simpler and more fulfilling life. The clutter in our homes can easily overwhelm us, affecting our mental and emotional state.

A minimalist home, on the other hand, provides a calming and peaceful environment, allowing us to focus on what truly matters in life.

However, creating a minimalist home doesn't have to be done all at once, and it certainly doesn't have to be a daunting task.

You can start by decluttering and getting rid of things you don't need. It is crucial to do this in a responsible way, consider donating to charity shops, using free cycle to give away items you don't need online, or using Gumtree (UK), Craigslist (USA), Facebook Marketplace or even selling on eBay and Vinted.

By decluttering and creating space, you free yourself from the physical and mental burden of too many material possessions. You may start with a small task, like a drawer or a closet, and build on it gradually. You will begin to notice how freeing it is to let go of things that no longer serve you.

Let's start with the room you probably spend most of your time in. Even if most of that time is spent sleeping!

Creating a minimalist bedroom and wardrobe:

Creating a Minimalist Capsule Wardrobe:

A minimalist capsule wardrobe is a collection of clothing items that are carefully selected to include only essential and versatile pieces, typically around 30-40 items or less.

The purpose of a capsule wardrobe is to simplify the process of getting dressed and to eliminate decision fatigue by creating a cohesive and interchangeable set of clothing items that can be mixed and matched to create a variety of outfits.

The focus is on quality over quantity, with a focus on timeless pieces that can be worn for years to come, rather than trendy or fast-fashion items that quickly go out of style.

Creating a minimalist wardrobe is a great place to start in creating a minimalist home. It can be challenging to let go of clothes that we have held onto for years, but it is essential to keep in mind that we don't need many clothes to live a happy life.

A minimalist wardrobe consists of only the clothes that we love and wear regularly, making our mornings much simpler and less stressful.

Steve Jobs, the late co-founder and CEO of Apple, was famous for his signature black turtleneck, jeans, and sneakers. He believed that by having a simple wardrobe, he could reduce decision fatigue and increase his productivity.

Having a capsule wardrobe can have several mental and philosophical benefits. Firstly, it can help make easy decisions and reduce the feeling of being overwhelmed by choice.

By having a limited number of items in your wardrobe, you simplify the process of deciding what to wear each day. This can help you to feel more confident in your choices and free up mental energy to focus on other things.

Additionally, a capsule wardrobe encourages a shift towards mindful consumption, where you buy less and make more considered choices about what you bring into your life.

This can help to reduce stress and anxiety around shopping and promotes a more intentional and sustainable approach to living.

Finally, a capsule wardrobe can help to promote a sense of clarity and simplicity in your life, which can have positive effects on your overall mental well-being.

having a capsule wardrobe also allows for a shift in mindset and a deeper sense of self-worth. It encourages individuals to determine their own value and worth rather than seeking validation or approval from others through their clothing choices.

By simplifying their wardrobe, individuals can break free from the constant need to keep up with the latest trends and fashions, and instead focus on developing their own personal style that reflects their values and personality.

This can lead to a greater sense of confidence and self-assuredness, as individuals are no longer relying on external factors to define their sense of self-worth.

Ultimately, a minimalist capsule wardrobe can help individuals embrace a more intentional and mindful approach to fashion and self-expression, promoting a greater sense of satisfaction and contentment in all areas of life.

With a minimalist capsule wardrobe, it is also a lot easier to keep tidy and on top of laundry.

To start creating a minimalist wardrobe, it is important to assess the clothes that we currently own.

This can be a daunting task, but it is necessary to take a critical look at each item in our closet and evaluate whether we truly love and wear it regularly.

It can be helpful to create three piles of clothes: keep, donate, and recycle.

The keep pile should only include items that we love and wear regularly, while the donate and recycle piles should be reserved for items that no longer fit, are damaged beyond repair, or simply do not bring us joy.

Once we have pared down our wardrobe to only the items that we truly love and wear regularly, it is time to focus on building a capsule wardrobe.

A capsule wardrobe consists of a small number of versatile pieces that can be mixed and matched to create a variety of outfits.

This typically includes neutral basics such as a white t-shirt, black pants, and a denim jacket, along with a few statement pieces such as a colourful blouse / patterned skirt or a nice shirt/jumper.

By focusing on quality over quantity and investing in timeless pieces that can be worn for years, we can create a wardrobe that is both stylish and sustainable.

When building a minimalist wardrobe, it is also important to consider the materials and production methods used to make our clothes. Fast fashion has a significant environmental impact and often relies on exploitative labour practices, so it is important to choose clothes that are made sustainably and ethically.

This might mean investing in higher-quality items that are more expensive upfront but will last for years, or choosing second-hand clothes from thrift stores or online marketplaces such as Vinted or Ebay.

Finally, it is important to maintain our minimalist wardrobe by regularly assessing our clothes and ensuring that we are only keeping the items that we truly love and wear regularly.

This might mean conducting a seasonal purge and donating or selling items that we no longer need, or simply being mindful of the items that we add to our wardrobe in the future.

Creating a minimalist wardrobe can have a significant impact on our daily lives. By simplifying our closets and focusing on quality over quantity, we can reduce decision fatigue and make getting dressed each day a more enjoyable experience.

Additionally, by choosing sustainable and ethical clothing options, we can reduce our environmental impact and support fair labour practices. It may take some time and effort to build a minimalist wardrobe, but the benefits are well worth it.

My personal journey into the world of minimalist living through a capsule wardrobe and how this benefited me:

Prior to embracing minimalism in my clothing choices, my life was marked by disarray and clutter. My laundry basket was perpetually overflowing, making it nearly impossible to locate my favourite T-shirts or pants when I needed them. It felt like I had more of a "floordrobe" than an actual wardrobe.

This chaotic state had persisted for as long as I could remember. However, as I observed the simplicity that minimalism brought to the lives of others, I realised where I had gone astray. In the span of a week, I decided to confront my closet chaos. I meticulously combed through all my clothing items—socks, pants, shoes, and activewear—and compiled a list of only the essentials I truly needed.

I placed everything I didn't absolutely love or need into recycling bags. In the end, I hauled four large sacks filled with clothes I had accumulated over the years to the nearby Salvation Army clothes bin. This bin serves the dual purpose of providing clothing for charity and recycling textiles that can't be used.

Today, everything I own and wear fits neatly into just three drawers and onto just 6 hangers in my wardrobe.

My collection consists of only six T-shirts that I can comfortably wear daily. I made the conscious choice to purchase a few new plain hemp tees to replace the old, uninspiring T-shirts that had previously cluttered my closet. It was astonishing to realise that among all those clothes, I didn't have a single piece that I felt 100% comfortable wearing every day in any situation.

In my top drawer, I've organized my underwear, socks, and pyjamas. The middle drawer houses my everyday attire, including T-shirts, jumpers, jeans, and joggers. My gym and football gear are neatly stored in the bottom drawer, along with a pair of running shoes and football boots. Hanging in my wardrobe are a couple of shirts, two nice jumpers, two suits, and a pair of shoes, all fitting snugly into the available space.

My aim wasn't to limit my clothing items to a specific number, as some minimalists do, but rather to ensure that all my clothes could be stored neatly in my available space while still offering enough options to avoid doing laundry more than once per week.

This shift to a capsule wardrobe not only streamlined my daily routine but also opened up physical and mental space that allowed me to embrace the broader principles of minimalism, simplifying not just my wardrobe but my life as a whole.

Creating a Minimalist & Sustainable Laundry Routine:

The benefits of a minimalist laundry routine are numerous.

First and foremost, it can save you time and energy. With fewer clothes to wash and fold, you'll spend less time doing laundry and more time on the things that really matter to you.

Additionally, having a simplified laundry routine can help you save money by reducing the amount of detergent, water, and electricity you use.

Finally, a minimalist laundry routine can help you reduce your environmental impact by cutting down on water and energy usage.

Creating a minimalist laundry routine starts with assessing your current habits and identifying areas where you can simplify.

One approach is to reduce the number of clothes you own, as discussed above, so you have less to wash and fold.

Another approach is to wash your clothes less frequently and wear t-shirts or daily outfits for as long as they feel fresh and clean, especially items like jeans and sweaters that don't need to be washed so often.

Simplify the laundry products you use. Instead of purchasing a variety of detergents, fabric softeners, and stain removers, choose one or two products that work well for your needs. You can also consider switching to eco-friendly and all-natural laundry products to reduce your environmental impact.

You can also use natural stain removers like baking soda or vinegar instead of harsh chemicals, and opt for air-drying your clothes instead of using the dryer. You can also replace your old detergents with natural eco alternatives at zero-waste refill shops if you have one locally.

It is also worth considering buying a laundry bag such as a GuppyFriend where you can store all your dirty activewear and polyester-based clothing to be washed without shedding microfibres from your clothes into the waterways via your washing machine as the Guppy Friend is designed to go in your washing machine to catch these microplastics.

As soon as your laundry is done, fold all your clothes up right away and put them back in their allocated spot. This simple habit will help keep your bedroom tidy and organised + it will be much easier once you have less stuff to put away and more space to put it in.

Another way to simplify your laundry routine is by designating specific laundry days.

Rather than doing small loads of laundry every day, set aside one or two days a week for doing laundry. The less, the better. This not only saves time and energy but also helps you establish a routine + ensures you always have enough clothes available, even with a small capsule wardrobe.

By incorporating these habits into your routine, you can create a minimalist laundry routine that works for you and helps you live a more intentional and sustainable lifestyle.

Creating a Minimalist Bedroom:

Creating a minimalist bedroom space can be a wonderful way to promote calmness and tranquillity in your home.

A minimalist bedroom is a sanctuary, a place where you can relax and unwind at the end of the day.

It is important to remove anything that is not essential to your bedroom, as this will help to reduce clutter and promote relaxation.

To create a minimalist bedroom, start by decluttering your space. Remove anything that does not belong in your bedroom, such as books, paperwork, or electronics.

Keep only the essentials, such as your bed, night stand, and perhaps a dresser or wardrobe. If choosing new furniture for your bedroom, opt for pieces that are simple and functional, without unnecessary embellishments or decorations.

As for electronics, remove anything that is not necessary for your sleep routine. This includes TVs, laptops, and tablets. Do you wake up and instantly check your phone or stay up on it all night? If so, consider leaving it in another room overnight.

The blue light emitted from electronic screens can disrupt your sleep patterns, so it's best to keep them out of the bedroom altogether. If you must have electronics in your bedroom, consider using blue light-blocking glasses and downloading a blue light-blocking app to help reduce the impact on your sleep.

When decluttering your bedroom space, you can go through your books and decide which ones to keep, donate, or sell. If you have books that you no longer need or want, consider donating them to a local library or charity. Alternatively, you can sell them online or at a yard sale.

As for paperwork and other items that don't belong in the bedroom, you can either relocate them to their proper places in your home or get rid of them altogether. If the paperwork is important, file it away in a designated folder or binder. If it's no longer necessary, shred it & recycle it.

For other items, consider whether they have a place in another part of your home or if they can be donated, sold, or discarded.

Remember, the goal is to create a minimalist space that promotes relaxation and tranquillity.

If you can and haven't already, invest in high-quality bedding and linens. Soft, comfortable bedding and sheets, like those made from bamboo lyocell, can help you to relax and feel more comfortable in your bedroom.

Choose neutral or calming colours for your bedding, such as white, grey, or beige, to create a serene and peaceful atmosphere.

Consider the lighting in your bedroom. Natural light is best, so if possible, choose window treatments that let in as much light as possible and leave curtains open during the day.

Avoid harsh overhead lighting, especially before bed and instead opt for soft, warm lighting that creates a cosy and inviting atmosphere. You can achieve this with lamps or wall sconces placed strategically around the room.

Finally, add a few finishing touches to your minimalist bedroom space to make it more than just a functional space but one that feels homely and brings you joy.

Consider incorporating elements of nature into your minimalist bedroom space. Plants, natural materials, and other natural accents can help to create a calming and restful atmosphere. Incorporating these elements can also help to create a sense of connection to the natural world, which is important for our overall well-being.

Adding a piece of artwork or a decorative pillow can add a pop of colour or personality. However, it is important to keep these decorations to a minimum, as too many can create clutter and disrupt the peaceful atmosphere you are trying to achieve.

Creating a minimalist bedroom can take some time and effort, but the result is a peaceful and calming space that promotes relaxation and restful sleep. By keeping only the essentials in your bedroom, choosing calming colours and lighting, and adding a few simple finishing touches, you can create a tidy, clutter-free minimalist bedroom that is a sanctuary in your own home.

Once this is done, it will be easy to keep on top of tidying as there won't be lots of clutter around to make a mess with.

Creating a Minimalist Bathroom:

Creating a minimalist bathroom is another excellent step towards creating a minimalist home.

It is easy to accumulate unnecessary products, such as expired toiletries, hotel toiletries, or multiples of the same product.

Simplifying your bathroom to only the products you regularly use will not only free up space but also simplify your daily routine.

To create a minimalist bathroom, start by going through all of your products and assessing which ones you regularly use and which ones you don't.

Expired products duplicates or ones you have never used should be responsibly disposed of. It's important to be honest with yourself and let go of products that you have been holding onto "just in case" or because they were gifts.

Once you have narrowed down your products to only the essentials, consider storage solutions that can help keep your bathroom organized and clutter-free.

Clear containers or baskets can be a great way to store products and keep them easily accessible. Consider investing in a shower caddy or a hanging organiser to keep everything in its place.

When it comes to decor, less is more. Consider a neutral colour scheme and minimalistic decor, such as a simple plant or a piece of artwork, to keep your bathroom feeling spacious and calming.

A clutter-free bathroom can create a more peaceful and relaxing environment, making it easier to unwind after a long day.

It's also important to establish a routine for keeping your bathroom tidy.

Make it a habit to put things away immediately after use, and to wipe down surfaces regularly to prevent build-up. By maintaining a minimalist bathroom and keeping it clean and tidy, you can create a sanctuary in your home that promotes relaxation and a sense of calm.

Establishing a routine for cleaning your minimalist bathroom can be a helpful way to keep it tidy and clutter-free. One way to do this is to set a regular cleaning schedule, such as once a week or every other day. By doing this, you'll be able to maintain a clean and minimalist bathroom without it becoming overwhelming.

Another tip is to keep cleaning supplies close at hand so that you can quickly clean up any messes as they occur.

A squeegee can be useful for wiping down shower walls after use to prevent soap scum build-up, and an eco-friendly cloth can be used to quickly wipe down surfaces after use. Only store the supplies you need and will use weekly to clean.

Additionally, it can be helpful to declutter your bathroom regularly to prevent unnecessary items from accumulating. Consider getting rid of expired products or products that you haven't used in a long time. This will not only free up space but also make it easier to clean and maintain your minimalist bathroom.

Remember, creating a minimalist home is not just about decluttering and organising. It is about creating a space that is functional, aesthetically pleasing, and conducive to a peaceful and mindful life.

By taking the time to simplify and declutter your home, you are creating space for the things that truly matter and freeing yourself from the burden of excess possessions.

Creating a minimalist kitchen:

Next, creating a minimalist kitchen can be a real game-changer.

It is easy to accumulate unnecessary gadgets, utensils, and cookware, but we can quickly cut down on these items by focusing on the essentials.

A minimalist kitchen consists of only the items that are regularly used in cooking and food preparation, creating a more streamlined and functional space.

It's important to take into account the size of your kitchen space and be realistic about how much you can fit in it without cluttering the area. The key is to focus on the essentials and only keep the items that you use regularly. This will create a more functional and streamlined space.

As an example more on the extreme side of minimalism, when travelling environmentalist Rob Greenfield managed to fit everything he owned into one backpack and just had one saucepan that he used for all his cooking + a metal spoon to eat with.

Of course, with a kitchen you don't need to be this minimalist but it really goes to show how little you actually need and is a great example of living within your means.

When creating a minimalist kitchen, it is essential to start by taking inventory of all the items in your kitchen.

Begin by decluttering and getting rid of any items that you no longer use or need. This can be a difficult process, as it can be tempting to hold onto items for sentimental reasons or because we think we may use them in the future. However, it is important to remember that every item in our kitchen takes up physical and mental space, and the more we have, the more cluttered and stressful our kitchen can become.

You can declutter kitchen items by either selling or donating them online or recycling them at your local recycling centre.

Once you have decluttered, focus on the essentials that you use regularly. This may include pots and pans, utensils, dishes, and appliances such as a kettle or toaster. Ask yourself, how many utensils, pots and pans do you really need?

An excellent resource for minimalist cooking in the kitchen is the search phrase 'one pot meals' or 'roast tins' as these require little equipment/effort and create little cleaning as well. Look these up and save your favourite recipes. We will dive deeper into creating a minimalist cooking routine in week 4.

Another key aspect of creating a minimalist kitchen is to focus on organisation.

Everything should have its place, and items should be stored in a way that is both functional and aesthetically pleasing. For example, use drawer dividers or organisers to keep utensils and cutlery in order, and store frequently used items in easily accessible locations.

This will not only make cooking and food preparation more efficient, but it will also create a sense of calm and order in your kitchen.

In addition, it's important to establish a routine for washing up and clearing clutter to keep a tidy kitchen. A tidy kitchen can make a big difference in how you feel about your home and your daily routine. Having a kitchen that is ready to use when you need it, without having to wash up old dirty pans or clear away clutter, can help you stay motivated and inspired to cook and prepare healthy meals.

One tip to keep in mind when creating a minimalist kitchen is to opt for multi-functional items. For example, instead of having a separate blender, food processor, and juicer, you can invest in a high-quality blender that can do it all. This will save you both space and money.

Another tip is to limit your storage space for kitchen items. Having too much storage space can encourage you to keep items that you don't need or use, leading to unnecessary clutter. Instead, consider using open shelving or hanging storage solutions to keep your kitchen essentials within reach and organised.

Remember, a minimalist kitchen doesn't mean you have to sacrifice functionality or style. It's all about finding the balance between what you need and what you truly love.

By keeping your kitchen space clear and organised, you'll find it easier to prepare healthy meals and enjoy your time in the heart of your home.

Finally, when it comes to creating a minimalist kitchen, it can be helpful to adopt a minimalist mindset when it comes to food and grocery shopping. Focus on buying only what you need, and avoid overstocking or buying in bulk unless it is essential.

This will not only help to reduce food waste, but it will also ensure that your kitchen remains clutter-free and functional. More on this in week 4!

By creating a minimalist kitchen, you will be able to enjoy a more streamlined and efficient space that is both functional and aesthetically pleasing.

It can take some time and effort to declutter and organise, but the benefits are well worth it. You will be able to save time and reduce stress in the kitchen, and you will also be contributing to a more sustainable and mindful way of living.

When creating a minimalist kitchen it can help to write a list of daily tasks somewhere visible i.e. on a whiteboard on the fridge.

Daily tasks can include washing dishes, drying and tidying items, mopping the floor and wiping down sides. Get into a habit of doing these things quickly before settling down to relax for the evening or heading out.

Listen to music or podcasts to make this a time you look forward to instead of a chore you dislike, and also focus on the peace of mind you feel when it's finished.

Final Touches to Your Minimalist Home

Finally, when it comes to creating a minimalist home, the key is to focus on the overall goal of simplicity and creating space. By gradually implementing minimalist habits and decluttering over time, you can create a home that brings you peace and tranquillity.

In addition to the bedroom, kitchen, and bathroom, there are other areas of the house that can benefit from minimalist practices.

The living room, for example, can easily become cluttered with unnecessary furniture, knick-knacks, and other items that don't serve a functional purpose. By removing items that are not essential and focusing on simple and functional decor, you can create a calming and relaxing space that promotes a sense of peace and tranquillity.

Stairwells and hallways are often overlooked areas, but they can also benefit from minimalist practices.

These spaces can quickly become cluttered with shoes, coats, and other items that are not in their proper place. By creating designated storage areas and minimising the amount of stuff that is stored in these spaces, you can create a more organised and streamlined home.

The porch or the first room of the house that greets you and your guests is essential to keep it tidy and clutter-free. Shoes, coats, and other items tend to accumulate in this space, leading to a cluttered and unwelcoming environment.

Creating a designated storage area for outdoor items such as shoes and coats can help to keep this area tidy and promote a sense of calm as you enter your home.

Outdoor spaces, including the garden, can also benefit from minimalist practices. Old plant pots, garden tools, or furniture that is no longer in use can quickly accumulate in the garden, leading to a cluttered and overwhelming space.

By regularly decluttering these spaces and creating a designated storage area for outdoor items, you can create an inviting and relaxing outdoor area that promotes a sense of calm and relaxation.

Apply the principles you have learned previously in this chapter when decluttering all other areas of your house and add them to your 12-week plan, ensuring they get taken care of by the end of the 12 weeks.

Overall, creating a minimalist home is a journey that requires time, patience, and dedication. However, by gradually implementing minimalist practices in each area of your home, you can create a space that brings you joy and a sense of peace.

Remember, the key is to focus on simplicity and creating space and to let go of anything that does not serve a functional or meaningful purpose in your life.

In summary, by adopting a minimalist mindset, you can declutter your home, free up physical and mental space, and reduce stress in your daily life.

Creating a minimalist home is a process that takes time, so don't be hard on yourself.

Start small and gradually build on your progress.

By the end of the 12 weeks, you will have incorporated 12 new minimalist habits into your life and created a home that sparks joy and simplicity.

Conclusion and Actionable Steps for Week 1

Congratulations on starting your journey towards a more minimalist home and life!

In Week 1, we will begin by making a clear decluttering plan and then start decluttering one small area of your home at a time.

This could be a single drawer, a closet, or a bookshelf. The goal is to start small and work your way up to larger areas of your home over the next 12 weeks.

Be gentle with yourself and your time. Don't overwhelm or stress yourself out but get everything you need to do out of your head and onto paper (or a digital planner).

With a clear plan, you will feel more at peace, knowing what needs to be done and when.

Here's a simple checklist of tasks to do during this challenge, starting this week to help create a minimalist home.

1. Create a plan:

Take out a notebook or planner and write down all the areas of your home that you want to declutter over the next 12 weeks. Break down each area into smaller tasks so that you have a clear idea of what you need to do in order to achieve your goal. This plan should be made with the advice in this chapter in mind. This plan will serve as a roadmap for the rest of the challenge.

2. Be honest with yourself:

As you go through each item in the area you're decluttering, ask yourself if it brings you joy or serves a purpose in your life. If not, add it to your declutter list for that area. Don't hold onto unwanted items for sentimental value if they're just causing clutter.

3. Schedule time:

Look at your schedule for the upcoming week and block off 15 minutes each day to work on decluttering. Start by tackling the areas that you've identified as the easiest to declutter or the ones that bother you the most.

4. Schedule bigger blocks of time for decluttering:

For example, if you have extra time such as an hour or even half a day free on a weekend, use that time to tackle a larger area of your home.

5. Start decluttering:

Begin by decluttering one area of your home. This could be a single drawer, a closet, or a bookshelf. The goal is to start small and work your way up. Set aside 15 minutes a day to declutter or go through items and decide whether or not you need to keep them.

6. Donate, sell, or recycle:

Once you've decluttered an area, decide what to do with the items you no longer need.

If they're in good condition, consider donating or selling them. If they're no longer usable, recycle them. Make sure to dispose of them responsibly.

6. Build the decluttering habit:

Make decluttering a daily habit. It can be as simple as decluttering one item a day or going through one small area of your home each day. The key is to make it a consistent part of your routine and stick to the plan you made.

After completing these steps you should have a clear plan of what to do.

To give you a clearer picture of what this could look like, I have created an example 12-week plan below.

Edit this to suit your own needs and come back to this at any point you need to in the 12-week program.

I recommend starting with the wardrobe as this is usually the most challenging for people and will free up the most time once it's finished.

Week 1 = Declutter your wardrobe & create a minimalist laundry routine

Week 2 = Declutter the bedroom & create a minimalist tidying habit of making the bed each morning

Week 3 = Declutter the bathroom & create minimalist cleaning habits

Week 4 = Declutter the kitchen & create a minimalist cleaning routine

Week 5 = Declutter the living room & create a minimalist tidying routine

Week 6 = Declutter the garage / garden & create minimalist maintenance routine

Week 7 = Declutter the garden / balcony

Week 8 = Go back over any unfinished rooms

Week 9 = Evaluate how your weekly house cleaning routine is going and adjust if needed

Week 10 = Reevaluate whether there's still anything left to declutter

Week 11 = Keep on top of tidying and keeping the house clutter-free

Week 12 = Declutter any remaining items you don't need to hold onto

Example week:

Week 1: Declutter your wardrobe & create a minimalist tidying routine

Monday = 15 minutes: Go through your underwear drawer and tidy. Work out how many of each item I need and only keep my favourite and essential items. Add all unneeded items to a recycling bag to donate to charity shops / clothes recycling.

Tuesday = 15 minutes: Go through my wardrobe and make a plan of what I really need and make a list of my favourite items to wear that bring me the most joy.

Wednesday = 15 minutes: declutter my wardrobe and add any clothes I don't need to a recycling bag for clothes recycling or donating to charity + make a bag of any items of value to sell on Vinted / Ebay.

Thursday = 15 minutes: Go through any sports / activewear and decide what I really need, what items I actually like to wear and what I don't - adding the unwanted items to my clothes recycling bags.

Friday = 30 minutes: List any items from my Vinted / Ebay bag for sale

Saturday = 30 minutes: Take items to charity or clothes recycling / Salvation Army bins

Sunday = 15 minutes: Make a new laundry routine based on my new minimalist capsule wardrobe and the advice in this chapter on laundry routines.

By starting with just a small area and making a plan, you're already taking the first steps towards creating a minimalist home and incorporating mindful minimalism into your daily life.

Remember, the goal is not to declutter everything in one go but to build the habit of daily decluttering and make it a part of your routine.

This approach of habit stacking and building upon small daily habits is much more sustainable and achievable in the long run, compared to attempting a complete overhaul of your living space all at once.

As you begin to declutter and simplify your living space, you'll start to experience the benefits of a minimalist lifestyle, such as reduced stress and anxiety, increased focus, and more mental clarity.

By incorporating the other habits in the 12-week program, you'll be able to extend these benefits to other areas of your life, creating a more intentional and fulfilling existence.

So don't get overwhelmed, take it one day at a time and remember that every small step counts.

By the end of the 12 weeks, you'll have made significant progress towards creating a minimalist home and cultivating mindful minimalism in your daily life.

Remember, creating a minimalist home is an ongoing process, and it's okay to take things one step at a time. The goal is to create a space that promotes calmness and relaxation while being functional and inviting. Good luck on your minimalist journey!

Week 2: Simple Scheduling & Prioritising

The Art of Saying No (and Yes)

In our modern world, it's easy to get caught up in the constant demands and expectations placed upon us by others and even ourselves.

We often find ourselves saying "yes" to everything, even when it doesn't align with our priorities or values, leaving us feeling overcommitted, overwhelmed, and unfulfilled.

Conversely, we may struggle with saying "no" to requests or invitations, fearing rejection or conflict.

Learning the art of saying "no" and "yes" is crucial in living a simple, intentional life. By setting clear boundaries and prioritising our time and energy, we can free ourselves from the stress and chaos of overcommitment and create space for the things that truly matter.

This week, we will explore the importance of saying "no" and "yes" and introduce simple scheduling and prioritising techniques that can help us live a more intentional life.

Learning to Say No

In today's fast-paced society, it can be challenging to say no. We feel like we're letting people down, or we're afraid of missing out on an opportunity.

Saying yes to everything can lead to burnout and overwhelm, which is why it's essential to learn how to say no.

One of the most powerful things you can do for yourself is to learn how to say no. It's easy to say yes, but it takes courage to say no.

When you say no, you're taking control of your life and your time. You're setting boundaries and protecting your energy. Saying no is a way to honour yourself and your values.

But saying no can be difficult. We're often afraid of disappointing others or being seen as selfish. We worry about what people will think of us. We might feel guilty for saying no, even when we know it's the right thing to do. Learning to say no takes practice, but it's worth it in the end.

One of the biggest obstacles to saying no is fear. We're afraid of the consequences of saying no, so we say yes instead.

We might worry that people will be angry with us, or that we'll miss out on an opportunity. But the truth is that saying no can be liberating. It frees up time and energy for the things that matter most to us.

Another obstacle to saying no is guilt. We feel guilty for saying no, even when we know we can't take on another project or commit to another event. But it's essential to remember that saying no is not selfish.

It's necessary to protect our time and energy and to honour our commitments to ourselves and our families.

Setting boundaries is a critical component of learning to say no. Boundaries help us protect our time and energy, and they prevent others from taking advantage of us.

Setting boundaries can be difficult, but it's an essential part of self-care. When we set boundaries, we're telling people what we will and won't tolerate, and we're taking control of our lives.

In conclusion, learning to say no is a powerful tool for living a slower, more intentional life. Saying no can be difficult, but it's essential for protecting our time and energy.

Overcoming fear and guilt and setting boundaries are all critical components of learning to say no. By learning to say no, we can create space for the things that matter most to us and live a more fulfilling life.

Learning to Say Yes

Learning to say yes can be just as important as learning to say no. It's about prioritising your values and goals and saying yes to opportunities that align with them.

When you say yes to everything, you can end up spreading yourself too thin and losing sight of what's truly important to you.

The first step in learning to say yes is to identify your priorities.

What are the things that matter most to you? Is it spending time with family and friends, pursuing a particular hobby, or advancing in your career?

By identifying your priorities, you can begin to say yes to opportunities that align with them and turn down those that don't.

It's also important to let go of FOMO (fear of missing out). In today's world of social media and constant connectivity, it can be easy to feel like you're missing out on something if you don't say yes to every opportunity that comes your way.

But the truth is, there will always be more opportunities. By focusing on what's truly important to you, you can say yes to the things that matter most and let go of the rest.

Saying yes to the right opportunities can also help you grow and develop as a person.

Whether it's taking on a new project at work or trying a new hobby, saying yes can help you step outside of your comfort zone and expand your horizons.

Of course, saying yes also means saying no to other things. This can be challenging, especially if you're used to saying yes to everything. But by setting boundaries and being honest with yourself and others, you can learn to say no in a way that feels authentic and true to your values.

One way to set boundaries is to establish clear guidelines for yourself.

For example, you might decide that you won't take on any new projects at work that require more than 10 hours of work per week.

Or you might decide that you'll only attend social events on weekends so that you have more time during the week to focus on other priorities.

In summary, learning to say yes is about prioritising your values and goals, and saying yes to opportunities that align with them. By letting go of FOMO, setting boundaries, and overcoming fear and guilt, you can say yes to the things that matter most and let go of the rest.

Saying yes to the right things for your own priorities can help you grow and develop as a person, while also allowing you to focus on what's truly important to you. Whether that's friends, family, work or play, learning to say yes and no will help you streamline your time management and commitments for a more balanced lifestyle.

Implementing Simple Scheduling & Prioritising

Implementing simple scheduling and prioritising can be a game changer when it comes to leading a slower and more intentional lifestyle. It can help you stay organised, focus on what matters most, stress less and free up time for yourself.

One way to implement this is to break down your schedule and to-do list into manageable chunks.

To begin with, make a list of everything that you need to do in a day or a week. Then, divide these tasks into different categories based on their level of importance.

This will help you focus on the essential tasks that need to be done first. For example, you may have some work-related tasks that are time-sensitive and need to be completed before anything else.

Another effective way to prioritise your time is to keep a minimalist diary. This doesn't mean that you have to write down every single detail of your day, but rather, you can focus on the important events and tasks that need to be accomplished.

You can set aside time each day or week to review your diary and make sure that you are on track with your goals and priorities.

It's also important to eliminate non-essential tasks from your schedule. This may include saying no to social events that don't align with your priorities, or delegating tasks to others where possible.

Learning to say no can be difficult, but it's essential if you want to focus on what's important and avoid burnout.

Implementing simple scheduling and prioritising is an essential step towards living a slower, more intentional life. Breaking down your schedule, identifying your priorities, and letting go of FOMO can help you maximise your time and energy.

Saying no, overcoming fear and guilt, and setting boundaries are crucial skills to learn if you want to prioritise your needs and values.

By maximising your time and energy, you can also make the most of your free time. This may include scheduling downtime to relax and recharge, or engaging in activities that bring you joy and fulfilment.

By prioritising what's truly important, you can make sure that you have the time and energy to do the things that matter most to you.

The Minimalist Diary

Keeping a minimalist diary can help you stay organised and focused on what's important.

This can be a simple notebook or a digital app that you use to keep track of your schedule and to-do list.

By keeping things minimal and focused, you can avoid feeling overwhelmed or stressed out by your schedule.

In addition to breaking down your schedule and to-do list, another effective method for implementing simple scheduling and prioritising is to block out specific times in your diary for different tasks and activities.

This can help ensure that you have enough time for the important things, while also leaving plenty of room for rest and relaxation.

For example, you might block out <u>6-7am</u> each morning for exercise/ meditation, followed by <u>7-8am</u> for breakfast and getting ready for work.

From <u>8am-12pm</u>, you could focus on your most important work tasks, and then take a 30-minute break for lunch.

After lunch, you could block out another 2-hour work session, followed by a 30-minute break for a snack or a quick walk outside.

Finally, you could block out 6-7pm for dinner and spending time with family or friends, and 7-9pm for a hobby or leisure activity before winding down for bed.

Of course, the example above will look different for different people. Write down what works for you and what your ideal day would look like, then adjust from there as you go, making tweaks until you get it right.

Don't expect it to be perfect or to get it right straight away. If your current work commitments make it challenging to fully embrace your ideal day, view it as a goal to work towards.

Take it one step at a time and devise a plan that allows you to progress without overwhelming yourself in the process. Remember, the journey is just as important as the destination.

If you can't make your ideal day work for you right now, you can still feel happy that you have figured out a plan to work towards it.

Try to find joy in the journey, embrace each moment, and let contentment fill your days. Remember true fulfilment lies not only in achieving your goals but also in cherishing the simple pleasures that surround you every day.

Keeping a minimalist diary can also be a useful tool for staying organised and maximising your free time.

Instead of filling your diary with every task and appointment, focus on recording only the most important and time-sensitive items. This will help you avoid becoming overwhelmed with an overly detailed schedule, and give you the flexibility to make changes and adapt as needed.

Remember, you are only one person, and you don't have to do it all. Embrace your limits, and you'll find freedom in letting go of unrealistic expectations.

When keeping a minimalist diary, be sure to prioritise self-care and leisure time as well. This might mean blocking out time for a weekly yoga class, a hike in nature, or simply some quiet time to read or relax.

By intentionally making time for these activities, you'll be more likely to follow through and prioritise your own well-being and happiness.

Overall, implementing simple scheduling and prioritising is an essential step in living a slower and more intentional lifestyle.

By breaking down your schedule, identifying what's truly important, eliminating non-essential tasks and blocking out time for work, family/friends and leisure, you can make the most of your time and energy and avoid burnout.

It's crucial to be kind to yourself and acknowledge that it's okay to prioritise and focus on what truly matters without feeling the need to take on everything at once.

Additionally, keeping a minimalist diary and prioritising self-care, can help you stay organised and focused on what's important, allowing you to live a more intentional and present life.

You have the power to ensure that you have plenty of free time to rest, recharge, and pursue the things that bring you joy and fulfilment.

Conclusion and Actionable Steps for Week 7

As we conclude Week 7 of our journey towards a simpler and more intentional lifestyle, we have learned about the importance of saying no and yes, and the power of simple scheduling and prioritising.

To begin practising simple scheduling and prioritising, start by breaking down your schedule and to-do list into manageable tasks.

Identify what tasks are truly important and essential to your values and goals, and eliminate non-essential tasks that drain your time and energy. By doing this, you will maximise your time and energy, and have more time to focus on what truly matters.

It's important to remember that saying no is not always easy, but it's a powerful tool that can help you set boundaries and prioritise your values and goals. Overcoming fear and guilt can be a challenge, but practising self-compassion and being honest with yourself and others can help you feel more confident in your decisions.

On the other hand, saying yes can also be powerful when it aligns with your priorities and values. Prioritising your values and goals can help you let go of the fear of missing out (FOMO), and focus on what truly matters in your life.

As you continue on your journey towards a simpler and more intentional lifestyle, remember to stay committed to practising simple scheduling and prioritising, and be kind to yourself along the way.

It's okay to make mistakes and have setbacks, but celebrating your progress and accomplishments can help keep you motivated.

Actionable steps for this week:

- Set aside time to break down your schedule and to-do list into manageable tasks

- Start a minimalist diary or planner to help you stay organised and on track. This can be a physical notebook or a digital tool, whichever works best for you. Use it to block out time for important tasks and appointments, as well as for relaxation and self-care.

- Prioritise your values and goals when deciding how to spend your time. Ask yourself what's truly important to you and focus on those activities first. This might mean saying no to certain commitments or social events that don't align with your priorities.

- Maximise your time and energy by batching similar tasks together and avoiding multitasking. This allows you to work more efficiently and with greater focus, leaving more time and energy for the things that matter most to you.

- Block out free time in your schedule to allow for rest and relaxation. This could be anything from taking a walk outside, reading a book, or simply sitting quietly and doing nothing. Remember, it's important to give yourself permission to rest and recharge, so you can show up fully for the things that truly matter to you.

Keep up the good work, and continue prioritising your values and goals.

Week 3: Cultivating Gratitude and Finding Happiness

This week, we will focus on cultivating gratitude in our lives. This is a simple yet powerful tool to incorporate on your journey towards minimalism.

Gratitude is the practice of acknowledging and appreciating the good things in our lives, no matter how small they may seem.

It can help shift our perspective from focusing on what we don't have to what we do have.

It can help you appreciate the little things in life and find joy in the present moment. This mindset can reduce stress and increase overall happiness.

Your task for this week is to start a gratitude journal. Each day, take a few minutes to write down three things you are grateful for.

They can be as simple as having a roof over your head, a warm bed to sleep in, or a good cup of coffee. By focusing on the positive, you will train your mind to see the good in every situation.

Gratitude journaling is a powerful tool that can help cultivate a minimalist mindset. By focusing on what we are thankful for, we shift our attention away from the desire for more and towards appreciation for what we already have.

This shift in perspective can help us recognise the abundance in our lives and reduce our desire for unnecessary material possessions.

Additionally, gratitude journaling can help us develop a deeper sense of contentment and fulfilment.

By intentionally focusing on the positive aspects of our lives, we create a sense of gratitude that can help us feel more fulfilled and satisfied with what we have.

This feeling of contentment can reduce the need for external validation or material possessions to bring us happiness.

Overall, incorporating gratitude journaling into our daily routine can help us develop a minimalist mindset and reduce our desire for unnecessary material possessions by teaching us to be happy with what we have, and not to always look externally for happiness.

Actionable steps for this week:

1. Keep a gratitude journal (digital or notebook)
2. Write down 3-5 things you are grateful for every morning, evening or both - these can be big or small things and it's ok to repeat the same things.

This simple practice helps you wake up, start the day with positive thinking, and go to bed thinking positively.

Doing this over time will ingrain a deep sense of gratitude within you for the things you already have.

Try to continue journaling and practising gratitude beyond this week and throughout the rest of this program.

It doesn't need to take more than a few minutes a day. And if you miss a day, **don't worry**, simply pick up where you left off. The goal is progress, not perfection.

Week 4: Minimalise Mind Clutter

Developing a Regular Meditation Practice

> "With meditation, you become a sensitised super-hero, completely in control, with endless possibilities at your fingertips." — *Tara Stiles*

With so many types of meditation out there it can be hard to know which one to focus on. There's guided, breathing, candle, breath-work and more meditations but will they work for you? And how long should you do them for to get the most benefits from the practice?

On my journey, I was lucky and found the most simple and effective form of meditation (one that can work for anyone) right away when watching a documentary on George Harrison from The Beatles.

Transcendental meditation, or TM for short, is a popular form of meditation that has gained widespread recognition for its numerous health benefits and easy-to-follow framework.

It is a form of mantra meditation that involves silently repeating a specific word or phrase, known as a mantra, to help calm the mind and induce a state of deep relaxation. This practice is said to help reduce stress, improve mental clarity, and promote overall well-being.

TM is based on an ancient Vedic tradition of mantra meditation that dates back over 5,000 years. This form of meditation is rooted in the belief that the universe and everything in it is made up of vibrations, including sound vibrations.

By using a specific sound, or mantra, as the focus of the meditation, practitioners can tune into these vibrations and achieve a state of deep relaxation and inner peace.

In this chapter, we will explore the benefits of mantra meditation and how to practice it effectively.

We will also discuss the similarities between TM and Vedic mantra meditation, and how this ancient practice has influenced the modern form of TM that is widely practised today.

The Easiest & Most Effective Form of Meditation

Transcendental Meditation (TM) is a form of meditation that has been practised for centuries but gained significant popularity in the West in the mid-20th century. It is a mantra-based meditation technique that involves the repetition of a specific sound or word to focus the mind and achieve a state of deep relaxation.

Compared to other types of meditation, TM is often considered the easiest and most effective form.

Studies have shown that TM has numerous benefits for both physical and mental health. It has been found to reduce stress and anxiety, lower blood pressure, improve sleep, and enhance overall well-being. In addition, it has been shown to increase brain function, improve cognitive abilities, and even reduce the risk of cardiovascular disease.

The science behind why TM works is still being researched, but studies have suggested that it helps to reduce activity in the sympathetic nervous system (which is responsible for the body's fight or flight response) and increase activity in the parasympathetic nervous system (which promotes relaxation and healing).

This shift in the body's nervous system activity is thought to be responsible for the many benefits of TM.

Compared to other types of meditation, TM has been found to be the most effective at inducing the state of deep relaxation necessary for the body to experience these benefits.

This is likely due to the simplicity of the practice - the repetition of the mantra helps to focus the mind and prevent distractions, allowing the individual to enter a state of deep relaxation more quickly and easily.

Some of the benefits of TM include:

- Reduced stress and anxiety
- Lowered blood pressure
- Improved sleep
- Enhanced overall well-being
- Increased brain function
- Improved cognitive abilities
- Reduced risk of cardiovascular disease

Given the numerous benefits of TM, it is a practice that is worth exploring for anyone looking to improve their physical and mental health. It is also a practice that is easy to integrate into your daily routine, with sessions lasting only 20 minutes and requiring no special equipment or training.

With regular practice, the benefits of TM can be felt in a relatively short period of time, making it a powerful tool for enhancing overall well-being.

In addition to the scientific evidence supporting the benefits of transcendental meditation, there are also countless examples of people who have experienced its positive effects first-hand.

One of the most famous groups of TM practitioners is The Beatles, who were introduced to the practice by Maharishi Mahesh Yogi in the late 1960s. They often credited TM with helping them to achieve creative breakthroughs and manage stress during their hectic touring and recording schedules.

George Harrison even wrote a song about his experience with TM called "The Inner Light," in which he describes the practice as a way to achieve bliss and connect with the divine.

These stories and many others demonstrate the transformative power of this simple yet profound meditation technique.

It is important to note that TM is a trademarked technique that can only be taught by certified TM instructors.

While I cannot teach you TM in this book, I can provide instructions on the more ancient but similarly simple practice of mantra meditation.

This practice involves repeating a specific sound or phrase, or mantra, to help focus the mind and achieve a deep state of relaxation.

Like TM, mantra meditation has been shown to have numerous physical and mental health benefits, including reduced stress and anxiety, improved sleep, and increased clarity of thought.

So while you may not be able to learn TM directly from me, you can still benefit from the similar practice of mantra meditation.

If you are interested in the experience of learning TM from an instructor I would highly recommend doing so, as I did over 9 years ago now.

Learning from an instructor helps you dive deeper into the technique, learn how it works and connects you to like-minded people for the duration of a weekend group course, and beyond if you wish to join their many retreats.

Paying for a course and dedicating time to learning the technique + forming a support network also means you will be more likely to stick with this practice.

I originally went along to help reduce my social anxiety but after 3 months of consistently meditating for 20 minutes, 2 times a day, I noticed greater benefits in all areas of my life that can only truly be explained through having the experience yourself.

Finding joy in the simple things becomes a lot easier with the peace of mind achieved through meditating consistently this way.

You can learn directly from the official Transcendental Meditation charity or from the Meditation Trust (if in the UK) who are made up of TM teachers who set up their own charity with the aim of making TM more affordable and accessible.

If you'd like to get started with mantra meditation right away however, read on!

How to Meditate with Mantra Meditation

Mantra meditation is a simple and effective meditation technique that involves the repetition of a word or phrase to calm the mind and focus your thoughts.

Here are the steps to get started with mantra meditation:

- **Choose a quiet space and a comfortable position:**

Find a quiet space where you won't be disturbed and sit in a comfortable position with your back straight and your hands resting on your lap. This could be on a comfortable chair, sofa or propped up in bed with a pillow, anywhere you find comfortable and relaxing.

- **Select a personal mantra:**

Choose a word or phrase that has no particular meaning to you, as this will prevent your mind from getting distracted by the meaning of the words. It could be a sound or a syllable that feels soothing to you. Some examples include "Om," "Shanti," "Aham Prema," or "Soham."

- **Start repeating the mantra:**

Close your eyes and start repeating the mantra silently and slowly to yourself. Focus on the sound of the mantra and let it fill your mind. When your mind starts to wander, gently bring it back to the mantra.

- **Meditate for 15-20 minutes:**

Aim to meditate for 15-20 minutes, twice a day. Usually once before breakfast when waking and once before dinner in the evening is best. Set a timer to avoid getting distracted by worrying about the time.

- **End your meditation gradually:**

When your meditation time is up, slowly stop repeating the mantra and take a few deep breaths before slowly opening your eyes. Take a moment to notice how you feel and be gentle with yourself as you transition back into your daily routine.

Mantra meditation is a powerful tool for reducing stress, improving focus, and promoting inner peace.

It's important to remember that it's a practice, so don't worry if you find it challenging to quiet your mind at first. With regular practice, you'll begin to experience the benefits of mantra meditation in your daily life.

Some days will feel harder than others to sit and focus on meditation and that's ok, that is normal.

As you continue to practice mantra meditation, you may begin to notice changes in your mood throughout the day.

You may feel calmer, more centred, and better equipped to handle stress and challenges as they arise.

It's important not to get too caught up in analysing these changes or trying to force them to happen.

Instead, simply allow yourself to experience the benefits of meditation as they come, and trust that the practice is having a positive impact on your overall well-being.

With regular practice, you may find that these changes become more consistent and profound, leading to a greater sense of peace and clarity in your daily life.

Carry on your day as normal and don't look for the changes, let them appear to you. You will notice more and more the deeper you get into your meditation journey.

Meditation doesn't change who you are, it helps you discover who you are more deeply by calming down the noise in your mind so all that's left are your purest thoughts.

> *"The thing about meditation is, you become more and more you"* - David Lynch

Aim for Two Meditations Per Day

Meditating for just 20 minutes, twice a day, using the mantra meditation technique is recommended as an optimal duration, offering benefits equivalent to spending hours on many other meditation practices.

Even if your schedule doesn't permit a full 40 minutes each day, you can still experience significant advantages if you start with meditations shorter than 20 minutes.

The enjoyable and straightforward nature of mantra meditation makes it more sustainable compared to other methods you may have attempted.

Many individuals leading hectic lives have noted that, surprisingly, dedicating 40 minutes a day to Transcendental Meditation seems to expand their available time. This is attributed to the heightened alertness and creativity experienced after meditation, resulting in increased efficiency and productivity in less time.

It is important to note that the benefits of meditation can vary from person to person, and it is ultimately up to each individual to determine the frequency and duration of their meditation practice that works best for them.

Remember, meditation is a practice, and it can take time to develop the habit and feel its benefits.

Be patient and compassionate with yourself, and try to make meditation a regular part of your routine to experience its positive effects.

Overcoming Common Challenges in Mantra Meditation

Mantra meditation may seem simple, but it can still present certain challenges to practitioners.

Here are some common issues people may face and some tips

for overcoming them.

Dealing with distractions and thoughts:

One of the biggest challenges in mantra meditation is dealing with distractions and thoughts that may arise during the practice. It's important to remember that these distractions are natural and normal.

Instead of trying to push them away or suppress them, simply acknowledge them and let them pass without judgment. You can also try to refocus your attention on your mantra or your breath once you realise your mind has wandered.

Maintaining consistency in practice:

Another common challenge is maintaining consistency in your meditation practice. Life can get busy, and it can be easy to let your practice slip.

One way to overcome this challenge is to schedule your meditation sessions like an important appointment or commitment in your day.

Try to set aside a specific time each day to meditate, and make it a non-negotiable part of your routine.

Addressing scepticism and misconceptions:

Finally, some people may face scepticism or misconceptions about meditation.

It's important to remember that this practice has been scientifically studied and has a proven track record of effectiveness.

If you encounter scepticism from others or have doubts yourself, try to focus on your own experience and results or consider talking to an experienced meditation teacher or mentor who can provide guidance and support.

Additional Tips for a Successful Mantra Meditation Practice

Incorporating meditation into your daily routine can help you maintain a consistent practice. Choose a time and place where you can meditate without interruption.

This could be before breakfast and again in the afternoon. It is important to make it a priority and treat it like any other important appointment in your day.

Maintaining a positive attitude and an open mind is essential for a successful meditation practice.

Recognise that meditation is a process and not a quick-fix solution. Keep an open mind to experience the benefits of meditation without any preconceived notions or expectations. Remember that meditation is a journey, and with consistent practice, you can achieve your goals.

Staying committed and consistent is crucial to your success

with mantra meditation. It is important to remember that missing one or two meditations does not mean you have failed. The most important thing is to get back on track as soon as possible and maintain a consistent practice.

Making meditation a daily habit can help it become an integral part of your life and help you reap the benefits of a regular meditation practice.

At times, you may not find meditation relaxing or convenient, and it might be challenging to sit for the recommended 20 minutes. However, this discomfort is a sign of why the practice will be beneficial for you.

Meditation helps us become more aware of our thoughts and emotions, even the uncomfortable ones and teaches us to observe them without judgment. This practice can be transformative and lead to a greater sense of inner peace and clarity.

Conclusion and Actionable Steps for Week 8

In conclusion, developing a regular mantra (or transcendental) meditation practice can provide a multitude of benefits for your mind, body, and overall well-being.

From reducing stress and anxiety to improving focus and creativity, the benefits are endless.

By incorporating the practice of mantra meditation into your daily routine, you can experience a greater sense of calm and inner peace.

To develop a regular mantra meditation practice, here are some actionable steps for this week:

- Find a quiet space and comfortable position where you won't be disturbed during your meditation practice.

- Choose a personal mantra that you will repeat silently to yourself throughout your meditation sessions.

- Practice meditation twice a day using the how-to guide in this chapter. Ideally 20 minutes before breakfast and 20 minutes in the afternoon or evening before dinner.

- Stay consistent and committed to your practice, even on days when it may be challenging.

- Incorporate mindfulness into your daily routine, such as taking a few moments to breathe and focus on the present moment.

Remember, the benefits of transcendental meditation are cumulative and may take time to fully experience.

Stay patient and open-minded as you explore this powerful technique. With practice, you can cultivate a deeper sense of inner peace, clarity, and focus in your daily life.

Week 5: Digital Detox - Downsizing Your Technology

In today's world, technology plays an essential role in our daily lives, from staying connected with friends and family to getting work done efficiently. However, the constant barrage of notifications, social media, and digital distractions can leave us feeling overwhelmed, stressed, and drained.

This is where the concept of a digital detox comes into play.

A digital detox is a conscious decision to disconnect from technology for a specific period to improve our mental and physical health.

Taking a digital detox is brilliant for freeing up time and mental clarity as social media is designed to be addictive, releasing dopamine (a feel-good chemical) in our brains every time we get a like or a notification.

This can lead to spending excessive amounts of time on social media, which can negatively impact our mental health, including increased anxiety, depression, and decreased self-esteem.

Therefore, taking a break from technology can help reset our minds, reducing our dependence on digital distractions and creating space for more meaningful activities.

In this weeks chapter, we'll discuss the importance of downsizing technology and provide tips and strategies for conducting a successful digital detox.

We'll explore how to identify and minimise digital clutter, manage social media, and create a healthier relationship with technology.

So let's dive in and learn how to reclaim control of our digital lives.

Identifying Your Technology Needs

Identifying your technological needs is an important step towards downsizing your technology.

It can be tempting to hold onto every gadget and device, but it's crucial to determine which technologies are essential to your daily life. By doing so, you can create a more intentional and focused approach to your technology use.

One helpful tip for determining necessary technology is to consider your daily routine and which technologies are required to accomplish essential tasks. For example, a laptop or desktop computer may be necessary for work, while a smartphone may be necessary for communication.

It is also important to consider the potential negative effects of certain technologies, such as social media apps, which have been shown to be addictive due to their impact on dopamine levels in the brain.

Examples of technology to consider decluttering may include old or outdated devices, duplicates of devices, or technologies that have been replaced by newer or more efficient versions.

By eliminating unnecessary technology, you can create more space in your home and in your mind.

Taking a break from these technologies through a dopamine detox can be a helpful reset for the mind.

A dopamine detox involves temporarily abstaining from highly stimulating activities to reset the brain's sensitivity to dopamine—a neurotransmitter associated with pleasure and reward.

This may include limiting exposure to activities which give quick hits of dopamine such as social media, video games, and excessive internet use. The goal is to reduce desensitisation to dopamine and cultivate a greater appreciation for simpler, more meaningful and satisfying dopamine-inducing activities such as completing a challenge, engaging in a creative pursuit or spending time with loved ones.

Many individuals find value in taking breaks from these quick stimulating dopamine hits to promote focus, productivity, and mental well-being.

It's advisable to approach such practices with a balanced perspective and consider individual needs and preferences.

Decluttering Your Digital Space

In today's digital age, we are constantly surrounded by technology, and it can be challenging to keep our digital devices organised.

A cluttered digital space can be just as overwhelming as a cluttered physical space, so it's essential to declutter our digital devices regularly.

Here are some ideas for decluttering your digital space:

Uninstall unused applications:

We often download applications that we end up not using. These applications take up valuable storage space on our devices, so it's important to regularly uninstall unused applications.

Delete old files:

We tend to accumulate files over time, including documents, pictures, and videos that we no longer need. Deleting old files not only frees up storage space but also makes it easier to find the files we need.

Organize digital files:

Organising digital files can help you find what you need quickly and easily. Create folders for different types of files and label them appropriately.

Clear out your email inbox:

Our email inboxes can quickly become cluttered with promotional emails, spam, and old messages. Go through your inbox and delete any unnecessary messages. You can also create folders to organise important emails.

Clean up your desktop:

A cluttered desktop can be overwhelming and make it challenging to find what you need. Create folders for different types of files and move them off your desktop.

By decluttering your digital devices, you can create a more organised and efficient digital space.

Here are some examples of unnecessary digital items that you can get rid of:

Old text messages and voicemails:

These take up valuable storage space and can be deleted.

Duplicate photos and videos:

We often end up with multiple copies of the same file, so it's important to go through and delete duplicates.

Unused bookmarks:

If you have bookmarks that you haven't used in a while, it's time to delete them.

Outdated software:

Outdated software can be a security risk and should be uninstalled.

By getting rid of unnecessary digital items, you can free up valuable storage space and improve the overall efficiency of your digital devices.

Suggestions for organizing digital space:

Use cloud storage:

Cloud storage is an excellent way to store files, and it also frees up space on your device. Popular cloud storage options include Google Drive, iCloud, and Dropbox.

Utilize software to organize files:

There are several software options available to help organise your digital files, such as Evernote and Trello.

Regularly back up your data:

Regularly backing up your data ensures that you don't lose important files in case of a device malfunction or other issues.

By implementing these suggestions, you can create a more organised and efficient digital space that will help you be more productive and reduce stress.

Establishing Healthy Digital Habits

As important as it is to declutter and downsize technology, it is also vital to establish healthy digital habits.

Our relationship with technology should be balanced and intentional, rather than overwhelming and all-consuming.

Establishing healthy digital habits can help us use technology in a way that serves us, rather than letting it control our lives.

One way to start establishing healthy digital habits is by setting boundaries and limiting screen time.

This could mean designating only certain times of the day to check emails or social media, turning off notifications, or even scheduling a designated digital-free day each week.

Creating a more balanced relationship with technology can also involve finding alternative ways to relax and unwind that don't involve screens.

Consider picking up a new hobby, spending more time in nature, or engaging in physical activity. By finding other ways to decompress, we can reduce our reliance on technology as a way to cope with stress or boredom.

Overall, establishing healthy digital habits is all about being intentional and finding a balance that works for you. By setting boundaries and finding alternative ways to unwind, we can create a healthier and more mindful relationship with technology.

Minimalist Phone

If you struggle with phone addiction, try downloading the app minimalist phone.

This helped me a lot personally, hiding social media apps and the infinite scroll of the swipe-right newsfeed that's full of endless clickbait.

Minimalist Phone is an app designed to help individuals overcome phone addiction and maintain a minimalist lifestyle.

The app allows users to simplify their phone interface by removing distractions such as app icons and notifications that can lead to excessive phone use.

The app also provides users with the ability to set usage limits for certain apps, track their phone usage habits, and schedule phone-free time.

I now use time Minimalist Phone time prompts which I set to either 5, 10, or 15 minutes when opening any social media app to remind me to 'exit this app' after that designated time period is up.

By setting boundaries and limits on phone usage, individuals can create a healthier and more balanced relationship with their phone and technology.

Furthermore, the app serves as a usual reminder for users to take breaks from their phone and engage in other activities such as exercise, meditation, or spending time with loved ones.

This helps individuals to not only reduce their phone usage but also to prioritise other important aspects of their life.

Overall, Minimalist Phone is a useful tool for those seeking to overcome phone addiction and create a more intentional and mindful relationship with their phone. By utilising the app's features and taking breaks from their phone, individuals can reduce their phone usage and improve their overall well-being.

I found this app perfect for finding a balance between social media use and being productive, without having to completely remove social media from my life. A balance I previously struggled to achieve for years.

Conclusion and Actionable Steps

In conclusion, downsizing your technology is an essential step towards creating a minimalist lifestyle that promotes mindfulness and balance.

By identifying your technological needs, decluttering your digital space, and establishing healthy digital habits, you can create a more intentional and purposeful relationship with technology.

Start taking action today and enjoy the benefits of a more mindful and balanced relationship with technology.

If you find yourself opening social media when you have some spare time, be mindful and ask yourself could you do something more fun and productive, an activity where you will feel better for doing it afterwards?

Remember, downsizing your technology is a process that takes time and effort, but the benefits of a more intentional and mindful relationship with technology are well worth it.

Start small and be consistent in your efforts, and you will soon see the positive impact it has on your overall well-being.

To start taking action this week, try the following steps:

- Identify your technological needs:

Take some time to assess your technology use and determine what is truly necessary and what can be eliminated. Be very honest with yourself here!

- Declutter your digital devices:

Take some time to go through your digital devices and delete any unnecessary items such as old apps, photos, and documents.

- Set boundaries and limits:

Consider setting a daily screen time limit for yourself and creating specific times of the day when you will not use technology or at least not look at a screen.

- Create a technology-free zone:

Consider creating a designated space in your home where technology is not allowed, such as your bedroom or dining area.

As a fifth step towards establishing healthy digital habits, try replacing some of the time you spend on technology with activities that promote mental health, such as spending time outdoors.

Go for a walk in the woods and listen to music, a podcast or just remove technology completely & instead **tune into the sounds of nature.**

Being in nature can help reduce stress, increase creativity, and improve overall well-being. By incorporating this into your weekly routine, you can create a better balance between technology use and other meaningful activities.

Week 6: Simplifying Your Diet & Nutrition

Mindful Eating and Meal Planning

Welcome to Week 6 of your minimalist habit stacking program.

In this chapter, we will focus on the important topic of mindful eating and meal planning, and how it can help simplify your diet and improve your overall health and well-being through good nutrition.

This is an important week for improving your clarity, peace of mind and ability to find the joy in simple pleasures, all through the practice of preparing and eating healthy food.

Mindful eating involves being present and aware of what you are eating, how you are eating, and how it makes you feel.

Meal planning, on the other hand, involves pre-planning and preparing meals in advance, which can help save time, reduce food waste, and ensure that you are consuming a balanced and nutritious diet.

Simplifying your diet through mindful eating and meal planning can have many benefits, including improved digestion and nutrient absorption, increased awareness of food choices and portion sizes, and reduced food waste and grocery costs.

In this chapter, we will explore the nutritional focus areas that you should consider, tips for simplifying your grocery shopping and meal planning, how to find joy in cooking and preparing healthy food, and mindful eating habits to incorporate into your daily routine.

It is worth noting in this chapter that you won't see me recommending meat or dairy as this would go against my own personal beliefs. I don't however want to come across as telling you how to eat, the choice is yours. However you choose to eat, the key minimalist steps such as meal planning and simplifying grocery shopping by focusing on whole unprocessed foods will work all the same.

By the end of this chapter, you will have actionable steps to start simplifying your diet, improving your relationship with food, and promoting better health and well-being.

Benefits of Mindful Eating and Meal Planning

Eating mindfully and planning your meals can offer several benefits for your physical, mental, and emotional well-being. Here are some of the most significant benefits of mindful eating and meal planning:

Improved digestion and nutrient absorption:

When you eat mindfully, you are more likely to chew your food properly and eat slowly, which can aid in digestion.

Additionally, planning your meals ahead of time can help ensure that you are getting a balanced diet with all the essential nutrients your body needs.

Increased awareness of food choices and portion sizes:

Mindful eating can help you develop a better understanding of your food choices, including their nutritional value and how they make you feel after eating them.

Planning your meals ahead of time can also help you control portion sizes and prevent overeating.

Reduced food waste and grocery costs:

Meal planning can help you reduce food waste by ensuring that you only buy what you need and use up all your ingredients before they go bad.

This can also lead to cost savings by minimising the amount of food you throw away and allowing you to take advantage of sales and discounts when shopping for groceries.

Nutritional Focus

Taking a minimalist approach to including essential nutrients in your diet means focusing on nutrient-dense foods that provide a high amount of essential vitamins, minerals, and nutrients with minimal processing or added ingredients.

This approach emphasises quality over quantity, encouraging you to choose foods that have the most nutritional value per calorie.

By focusing on essential nutrients, you can simplify your meal planning and reduce food waste by avoiding unnecessary or overly processed foods. This not only benefits your health but also helps you live a more minimalist lifestyle by promoting intentional and purposeful food choices.

When it comes to including essential nutrients in your diet, think about the foods that provide the most nutrients per calorie.

For example, dark leafy greens such as kale, spinach, and collard greens are excellent sources of calcium, iron, and other essential vitamins and minerals.

Legumes, such as lentils and chickpeas, are high in protein, fibre, and complex carbohydrates, making them a nutritious and filling addition to any meal.

Nuts and seeds, including chia seeds, almonds, and sunflower seeds, are rich in healthy fats, protein, and other essential nutrients.

Overall, taking a minimalist approach to nutrition means focusing on the essentials and avoiding unnecessary or overly processed foods. This not only promotes better health but also helps simplify your life by encouraging intentional and purposeful food choices.

Focusing on essential nutrients can help simplify your diet and ensure that your body is getting the necessary vitamins and minerals it needs to function properly. Here are 4 essential areas of nutritional focus that can help support a healthy diet:

1. Gut Health:

The health of your gut microbiome is crucial for maintaining overall health and wellness. The gut contains trillions of microorganisms that play a role in digestion, nutrient absorption, and immune function.

Incorporating foods that promote the growth of beneficial bacteria, such as fermented foods and probiotic-rich foods, can help improve gut health and reduce the risk of digestive issues, inflammatory conditions, and even mental health disorders.

The gut is often referred to as the "second brain" due to its close connection with our mood and overall health. This is because everything we eat is broken down and processed by the gut, and the nutrients that are absorbed can affect the rest of the body, including the brain.

The gut and brain are closely connected, and the health of one can affect the other. A healthy gut can lead to better mood, improved cognitive function, and even reduce the risk of neurological diseases.

A well-maintained gut can help prevent chronic illnesses such as heart disease and cancer, as well as reduce inflammation in the body. Additionally, it can aid in maintaining a healthy weight. As such, focusing on gut health can be a crucial area of nutrition for anyone who wants to improve their health and feel better.

By prioritising gut health, we can simplify our approach to nutrition and eliminate a lot of unnecessary complexity.

To learn more about this consider reading "Fiber Fueled" by Will Bulsiewicz, the Gut Health MD, for helpful insights and meal ideas that are good for your gut.

By incorporating fermented foods like sauerkraut and kimchi, as well as probiotic-rich foods like yoghurt and kefir, we can promote a healthy gut microbiome.

Eating plenty of fibre-rich whole foods like fruits, vegetables, and whole grains can also support gut health and help to keep the digestive system functioning smoothly.

By focusing on gut health, we can improve our overall well-being and reduce the risk of various health issues.

This simple approach to nutrition can help to streamline our grocery shopping and meal planning, making it easier to maintain a healthy diet. So, consider making gut health a key focus area in your nutrition journey, and explore resources like "Fiber Fueled" for inspiration and guidance.

2. Brain Foods:

The brain is responsible for controlling many bodily functions, and keeping it healthy is crucial for overall health and well-being.

Consuming a diet that is rich in nutrients, particularly those that support brain health, can have a significant impact on cognitive function and reduce the risk of developing neurological disorders.

Omega-3 fatty acids, found in foods such as flaxseeds, chia seeds, and walnuts, are particularly important for brain health.

These healthy fats have anti-inflammatory properties, which can help to protect the brain from damage caused by inflammation. Additionally, omega-3s are involved in the production of neurotransmitters that regulate mood and cognitive function, making them essential for maintaining good mental health.

Leafy greens, berries, and dark chocolate are also rich in antioxidants and other nutrients that support brain function.

Antioxidants help to protect the brain from damage caused

by free radicals, which are unstable molecules that can cause oxidative stress and damage to cells.

In addition to antioxidants, leafy greens and berries contain vitamins and minerals that support brain function, such as vitamin K, folate, and vitamin C.

Dark chocolate also contains flavonoids, which have been shown to improve cognitive function and reduce the risk of cognitive decline.

In addition to the physical benefits of a healthy brain, consuming nutrients that support brain health can also lead to improvements in mood, clarity, energy, and peace of mind.

For example, consuming omega-3 fatty acids can help regulate mood by influencing the production of neurotransmitters such as serotonin and dopamine, which are associated with feelings of happiness and well-being.

In addition, antioxidants found in foods such as leafy greens and berries can help reduce inflammation in the brain, which has been linked to depression and other mood disorders.

Furthermore, consuming foods rich in nutrients such as B vitamins, magnesium, and iron can also have a positive impact on brain function and mood.

These nutrients are involved in the production of energy and the regulation of hormones that affect mood and stress levels.

For example, low levels of B vitamins, particularly vitamin B12, have been linked to symptoms of depression and anxiety. Consider a B12 supplement if you're not eating foods fortified with B12.

Additionally, consuming foods rich in magnesium, such as nuts, seeds, and leafy greens, has been shown to reduce symptoms of anxiety and improve overall mood.

Incorporating these brain-boosting foods into your diet can be simple and delicious. Try adding flaxseeds or chia seeds to your morning smoothie or oatmeal, incorporating leafy greens and berries into your salads or snacks, and enjoying a piece of dark chocolate as an afternoon treat.

By making these small changes, you can support your brain health and improve your overall well-being.

In summary, focusing on brain health through a nutrient-rich diet can have numerous benefits for both physical and mental well-being, including improvements in cognitive function, mood regulation, and overall energy levels.

3. Essential Vitamins:

Vitamins and minerals are essential nutrients that the body needs to function properly.

Consuming a variety of whole foods that are rich in vitamins and minerals, such as leafy greens, fruits, and vegetables, can help ensure that your body is getting the nutrients it needs to support a healthy immune system, strong bones, and other important bodily functions.

Some essential vitamins that everyone needs for good health include vitamin A, vitamin C, vitamin D, vitamin E, vitamin K, and B vitamins (including thiamine, riboflavin, niacin, vitamin B6, folate, and vitamin B12).

These vitamins play important roles in various bodily functions, such as supporting the immune system, maintaining healthy skin and eyes, and aiding in the metabolism of carbohydrates, proteins, and fats.

It's important to consume a variety of fruits, vegetables, whole grains, and other nutrient-dense foods to ensure adequate intake of these essential vitamins.

4. Protein and Amino Acids:

Protein and amino acids are the building blocks of the body and are necessary for building and repairing tissues, maintaining muscle mass, and supporting immune function.

Plant-based sources of protein, such as lentils, beans, tofu, tempeh, quinoa, nuts, and seeds, are excellent sources of amino acids and can provide all the protein and nutrients that the body needs to function properly.

Focusing on plant-based sources of protein can also help

reduce the environmental impact of your diet and support a more sustainable food system.

One minimalist hack (apart from using protein powders) to hit your protein requirements each day is to use quinoa for a base of one or more of your meals.

Quinoa is a popular plant-based protein source and is often considered a complete protein because it contains all nine essential amino acids necessary for building and repairing tissues in the body. However, some other plant-based protein sources, such as beans or lentils, may not contain all of the essential amino acids on their own.

By combining these other protein sources with quinoa, you can create a complete protein source. For example, a quinoa and black bean salad can provide all the essential amino acids your body needs. Other combinations that work well include quinoa and lentils, quinoa and chickpeas, or quinoa and tofu.

Not only does combining plant-based protein sources with quinoa provide a complete source of protein, but it can also increase the variety of nutrients in your diet.

This is important for overall health, as different protein sources contain different vitamins and minerals. For example, quinoa is a good source of iron, magnesium, and zinc, while hemp seeds are a great source of omega-3s, and beans and lentils are rich in folate and potassium.

Incorporating a variety of plant-based protein sources into

your diet, including quinoa, and combining them to create complete proteins can provide your body with the essential amino acids it needs for optimal health.

If you struggle to plan all of these into your meals then you could try a daily multivitamin such as the plant-based multivitamin & omega-3 DHA algae oil by Vivo Life.

One simple way to ensure that you are incorporating all four of these key nutritional focus areas into your meal plans and shopping lists is to focus on whole, plant-based foods.

By limiting processed foods and artificial ingredients and increasing your intake of foods of high nutritional value such as fruits, vegetables, legumes, nuts, and seeds, you can naturally support gut health, brain function, and essential nutrient intake.

Additionally, planning ahead and prepping meals in advance can help you make healthy choices throughout the week and reduce food waste.

Consider cooking in bulk and freezing leftovers for easy and convenient meals, and try to use up all of the ingredients you purchase to reduce waste.

Tips for Simplifying Your Grocery Shopping

Simplifying your grocery shopping is an essential part of living a minimalist lifestyle. By limiting processed foods and artificial ingredients, you can reduce the amount of clutter in your pantry while also supporting your health.

One approach to simplify your grocery shopping is to focus on purchasing whole, fresh ingredients that you can use to make simple meals. This approach emphasises plant-based meals, which tend to be more affordable and nutrient-dense.

By avoiding pre-packaged meals, you can also limit the amount of waste you generate from packaging and food that goes unused.

Meal prepping and planning ahead can help you stay on track with your healthy eating goals, while also reducing the amount of time you spend cooking during the week. You can save time by cooking in bulk and saving leftovers for future meals.

By planning your meals ahead of time, you can also make sure you list all the necessary ingredients you need for the week, you can then get everything you need in one trip, reducing the need for multiple trips to the grocery store and wasted food items that you don't use in your meals before they go off.

Another way to simplify your grocery shopping is to shop seasonally and locally and then look up recipes to make using the ingredients you find. This approach can help you stay connected to your community while also supporting local farmers and reducing food miles.

When you shop seasonally, you can also take advantage of the freshest, most nutritious ingredients available. This is also a great step to take for learning to enjoy simple pleasures and finding more meaning in life, rather than seeing shopping as a chore but something that can be enjoyable and an uplifting experience as you support your own health whilst also supporting local and organic farmers.

Ultimately, simplifying your grocery shopping is about finding ways to reduce clutter, save time, and focus on the healthy foods your body needs.

By limiting processed foods, incorporating more plant-based meals, and planning ahead, you can simplify your meals while also supporting your health and wellness.

Meal Planning Tips

Meal planning can be a game-changer when it comes to simplifying your life and achieving your nutrition goals. By taking the time to plan out your meals for the week, you can ensure that you are eating healthy, balanced meals that meet your dietary needs and preferences. Here are some tips to help you get started with meal planning:

Identifying your dietary needs and preferences:

The first step in meal planning is to identify your dietary needs and preferences. This includes any allergies or food sensitivities you may have, as well as any specific diets you are following.

Once you have a clear understanding of your dietary needs, you can start planning meals that meet those needs while still being delicious and satisfying.

Planning meals around seasonal and local produce:

Incorporating seasonal and local produce into your meal planning is not only good for your health but also for the environment and your budget.

Seasonal produce is often less expensive and more flavourful, and buying locally supports small farmers in your community.

Creating a grocery list and sticking to it:

Once you have your meals planned out, create a grocery list of the ingredients you will need for the week.

Stick to your list when you go grocery shopping to avoid impulse purchases and unnecessary spending. This can also help reduce food waste by ensuring you only buy what you need.

Incorporating variety and trying new recipes:

Eating the same meals week after week can get boring, so make sure to incorporate variety into your meal planning. Try new recipes, experiment with different cuisines, and switch up your protein sources each week to keep things interesting.

By incorporating these meal planning tips into your routine, you can simplify your life, improve your health, and achieve your nutrition goals. With a little bit of planning and preparation, eating healthy and delicious meals can be easy and enjoyable.

How to Meal Plan:

Meal planning can seem like a daunting task at first, but with the right tools and strategies, it can actually be a time-saving and stress-reducing activity.

One helpful tool for meal planning is a meal planner or journal. This can be a physical notebook or an app on your phone, depending on your preference.

To structure your meal planner, start by dividing the journal into sections for each day of the week. Then, list out the meals you plan to eat each day, including breakfast, lunch, snacks and dinner. Be sure to take into account your dietary needs and preferences, as well as any seasonal or local produce that you want to incorporate.

Once you have your meal plan for the week, it's time to create a shopping list. Using a meal planner can help make this process more efficient, as you can easily see what ingredients you need for each meal.

To save time, consider keeping a folder of your favourite recipes either online, on your phone or in a physical folder stored in your kitchen. This can be a go-to treasure of a resource when it's time to plan your meals for the week.

To make the most of your meal planner and minimise the time spent on meal planning each week, set aside a designated time each week to plan your meals and create your shopping list.

This can be as simple as spending 20 minutes on a Sunday evening to plan out the week ahead. By creating a routine and sticking to it, you can make meal planning a seamless and stress-free part of your week.

Here are some tips on where to find meal planners for different preferences:

a) Digital meal planners on Etsy:

Etsy is a great place to find digital meal planners that you can download and print out at home. Many of these planners are customisable and can be tailored to your specific dietary needs and preferences.

b) Physical meal planners online:

If you prefer a physical meal planner, Etsy and other indie online stores also offer a variety of options. Some of these planners come with additional features like recipe pages and grocery lists and can be a helpful tool for keeping track of your meals.

c) Phone/tablet app meal planners:

If you prefer to use a digital meal planner on your phone or tablet, there are several options available. Some popular ones include Whisk, Mealime, Plan to Eat, and Cookpad. These apps can help you plan your meals, generate shopping lists, and even suggest recipes based on your preferences.

d) Forks Over Knives (paid but done-for-you meal planner):

For those who prefer a done-for-you meal planning service, Forks Over Knives offers a paid meal planner that provides weekly menus, grocery lists, and recipes based on a whole-food, plant-based diet. This service can be a great option for those who are short on time or prefer a more structured approach to meal planning.

Finding Joy in Cooking and Preparing Healthy Food

Cooking and meal preparation can often feel like a chore, but it's important to remember that it doesn't have to be that way. In fact, finding joy in cooking and preparing healthy food can make the experience more enjoyable and can lead to better health outcomes.

One way to enjoy the process of cooking is to view it as a creative outlet.

Cooking allows you to experiment with different ingredients, flavours, and techniques to create something unique and delicious. Don't be afraid to try new things and get creative with your meals.

Another way to find joy in cooking is to make time and space for it.

This can be challenging in our busy lives, but setting aside dedicated time for meal preparation can make a big difference.

Consider scheduling a specific day and time each week to plan and prepare meals. Also, create a clean and organised space to cook in, as this can make the process feel less chaotic and more enjoyable.

When it comes to finding inspiration and motivation to cook at home, there are many options.

Some people find inspiration in cookbooks, food blogs, or social media. Others find inspiration in the ingredients themselves, such as seasonal produce or local specialities.

Some people find motivation in the health benefits of cooking and eating at home, such as reducing the risk of chronic diseases and improving overall well-being.

In addition to these tips, there are many resources available to help make cooking and meal preparation more enjoyable.

Online cooking classes, cooking blogs, and social media can

provide inspiration and new ideas. Meal kit delivery services can also be a great option for those who want to simplify the meal preparation process.

Remember, cooking and meal preparation doesn't have to be a daunting task. By finding joy in the process, making time and space for it, and finding inspiration and motivation, you can create healthy and delicious meals that will nourish both your body and soul.

Mindful Eating Habits

Mindful eating is an approach that involves paying attention to your food, and the experience of eating. This practice can have many benefits, including increased enjoyment of food, reduced overeating, and improved digestion.

By taking a few simple steps, you can learn to eat more mindfully and make healthy eating a more enjoyable experience.

Eating slowly and mindfully

1. Taking the time to savour your food and eat slowly can help you enjoy the taste of your food more + feel more satisfied with a reduced urge to overeat. Eating slowly allows your body to register when it is full, preventing overconsumption.

Listening to your body's hunger and fullness cues

1. Tuning into your body's hunger and fullness signals can help you make healthier choices and avoid overeating. Eating when you are hungry and stopping when you are full can help you maintain a healthy weight and improve your overall health.

Reducing distractions during meals

1. Eating without distractions, such as TV or your phone, can help you focus on your food and the experience of eating. This can help you tune in to your body's hunger and fullness cues and reduce the urge to overeat.

Wash up as you go

1. Cleaning as you cook and washing up as you finish your meal can help create a more peaceful and mindful atmosphere in the kitchen. This can also help reduce the stress created further down the line by a stack of dishes to wash.

By incorporating mindful eating habits into your daily routine, you can learn to enjoy your food more fully, eat more healthily, and reduce the urge to overeat.

Putting It into Practice: Actionable Steps

Changing your eating habits and incorporating new healthy behaviours can be challenging.

It requires commitment, persistence, and the willingness to step outside of your comfort zone. However, it is also incredibly rewarding and can lead to significant improvements in your health and well-being.

Here are your actionable steps to take from this week to implement mindful eating habits into your daily routine.

- Make a Healthy Meal Plan and Shopping List for This Week

Use a meal planning app, planner or template and make a healthy meal plan and shopping list for this week. This will help you stay organised and save time and money by reducing food waste and preventing impulsive purchases.

Plan at least 1 day where you will eat only whole (unprocessed) foods for the whole day. Next week plan 2 days like this and keep going until you're at 7.

- Experiment with new recipes and ingredients

This helps to keep your meals interesting and satisfying. Don't be afraid to try new foods or cuisines, and seek out inspiration from cookbooks, online resources, or cooking classes.

When you find meals you love, store them all in one place such as a folder in the kitchen or on your phone/tablet, for easy reference when weekly meal planning.

Make sure to list a good amount of easy meals that are quick to make i.e. under 10 minutes prep, if you don't like spending too much of your time in the kitchen.

I personally found my balance in planning around 5 easy but delicious meals a week then just 1 or 2 nights where I'll spend time in the kitchen cooking up something new and more adventurous to keep things exciting.

- Practice Mindful Eating Habits

Try to remember to eat slowly, listen to your body's hunger and fullness cues, and reduce distractions when eating meals.

This can help you enjoy your food more, improve digestion, and prevent overeating.

By incorporating these actionable steps into your daily routine, you can create sustainable habits that support a healthy and balanced lifestyle. Remember to start small, be patient with yourself, and celebrate your progress along the way.

You can use habit stacking to make these actionable steps easier to implement.

For example, you can incorporate meal planning and mindful eating into your weekly routine by making them new habits.

Start by committing to creating a healthy meal plan and shopping list every week. Then, the next week set aside an hour twice per week to meal prep lunches for the next 3-4 days.

By habit stacking in this way, you'll find that healthy eating becomes second nature, and you'll be well on your way to a healthier, happier you.

Don't expect to have the perfect meal plans and be mindfully eating at every meal right away, just make a start this week and you will get better at these things over time.

Conclusion

Simplifying your diet through mindful eating and meal planning can lead to numerous benefits, such as improved digestion, better mood, and increased energy levels.

By implementing small changes and making healthy eating habits a part of your daily routine, you can achieve a healthier and happier lifestyle.

I encourage you to continue making positive changes to your diet and prioritising your health and well-being.

Week 7: Creating a Minimalist Budget

Simplifying Your Finances

Having a minimalist budget & mindset can be a powerful tool for achieving financial freedom and thus reducing stress.

By simplifying your finances, you can gain a better understanding of your spending habits, prioritise your expenses, and live a more intentional life.

In this chapter, we will explore the importance of creating a minimalist budget and the financial benefits that a minimalist philosophy can bring to your life.

Financial Freedom through Minimalism: The Psychology and Philosophy of Spending Less and Living More

The psychology and philosophy behind needing less to find happiness lies at the heart of minimalism. As everyone wants and deserves happiness, this realisation is therefore essential whether you are struggling financially or not.

> *"Money is numbers and numbers never end. If it takes money to be happy, your search for happiness will never end"* - Bob Marley

In a world often driven by consumerism and the pursuit of more, minimalism provides a refreshing perspective. It challenges the notion that material possessions equate to happiness and instead emphasizes the value of **experiences, relationships, peace of mind** and **personal growth**.

From a psychological standpoint, studies have shown that the pursuit of material wealth often leads to a paradoxical decline in well-being. Constantly chasing after more can create stress, anxiety, and a sense of emptiness.

Minimalism, on the other hand, encourages individuals to declutter their lives, both physically and mentally, by shedding the excess and focusing on what truly matters. This process can lead to reduced stress, improved mental clarity, and a greater sense of contentment.

From a philosophical perspective, minimalism aligns with various schools of thought that emphasise the importance of simplicity and mindfulness.

Philosophers like Epicurus and Henry David Thoreau extolled the virtues of a simple life centred on personal reflection and meaningful connections.

Minimalism echoes these sentiments by encouraging individuals to detach from the relentless pursuit of possessions and embrace the art of intentional living.

It invites us to question societal norms and find happiness in the freedom of owning less.

In essence, needing less is a pathway to a deeper, more profound form of happiness. It invites us to savour life's simple pleasures, cultivate gratitude, and prioritise what truly enriches our existence.

Minimalism challenges us to free ourselves from the constant craving for more, allowing us to discover contentment and fulfilment in the present moment.

Living Within Your Means and Finding Fulfilment

Simplifying your budget is a fundamental step toward living a more minimalist and fulfilling life. It's about allocating your resources intentionally and finding contentment in what truly matters.

Here's how you can create a budget that aligns with minimalist values and helps you avoid working extra hours to cover unnecessary expenses:

1. Identify Needs vs. Wants:

Begin by categorising your expenses into needs and wants. Needs include essential items like housing, food, utilities, and transportation. Wants are non-essential items or services that add convenience or luxury but may not contribute significantly to your happiness. Focus on reducing or eliminating wants to free up resources.

2. Cut Unnecessary Expenses:

Review your spending habits and identify areas where you can cut back. This might involve cancelling unused subscriptions, cooking at home instead of dining out frequently, or buying second-hand items instead of new ones. Every dollar saved is one less you need to earn.

3. Embrace Minimalist Purchasing:

Adopt a minimalist approach to shopping. Ask yourself if an item adds real value to your life before making a purchase. Avoid impulse buying and give careful thought to each expenditure. This practice not only saves money but also reduces clutter and stress associated with excess belongings.

4. Set Clear Financial Goals:

Establish clear financial goals that align with your minimalist values. This could include saving for experiences like travel, investing in quality over quantity, or building an emergency fund to reduce financial stress. Having specific goals provides motivation and direction for your budgeting efforts.

By simplifying your budget, you can live comfortably within your means, reduce financial stress, and avoid the need to work extra hours to cover unnecessary expenses.

This financial freedom allows you to pursue a more minimalist and fulfilling life centred on experiences and meaningful choices rather than material possessions.

To illustrate how this concept applies in real life, consider the following scenario:

You have a baby boy, and in the excitement of parenthood, you're determined to provide him with all the happiness in the world. You want to offer him the best experiences and gifts possible. However, your current job doesn't easily accommodate these desires. So, you set out to devise a plan to generate the necessary income.

Eventually, you realise that you can indeed afford everything you've envisioned. You can take your son to Disneyland by the time he's four years old, and buy him all the latest toys and stylish clothes you've dreamed of. However, achieving this requires doubling your weekly working hours, which means sacrificing the evenings you could spend playing with your son as he grows up.

The question arises: Is it worth it? Or might it be better to live in the present moment and not miss out on his childhood by working excessively? Instead, you can savour the simple pleasures that enrich your lives—outdoor adventures, quality time together at the park, or visits with friends.

These experiences cost nothing but offer invaluable life lessons, teaching your child contentment with what they have.

This doesn't mean you should abandon your dream of taking them to Disneyland; experiences are indeed valuable and can be pursued.

You could also speed up the process of saving up for that trip if you cut back on buying unnecessary items, that are wants not needs, such as buying him designer clothes or going for expensive trips outside of your financial means, when you could instead do something that is fun and free or inexpensive.

The point of this exercise is to assess whether achieving it currently necessitates such a substantial sacrifice of your present time—a sacrifice that can never be reclaimed, regardless of your financial gains.

We'll delve deeper into goal setting and strategies for maximising your earnings and free time in next week's minimalist challenge.

Assessing Your Current Financial Situation

A minimalist budget starts with assessing your current financial situation. This involves understanding your income and expenses and identifying areas where you can cut back on spending.

You can begin by gathering all your financial statements and bills to create a clear picture of your current financial standing.

Next, review your expenses on your statements and categorise them into essential and non-essential expenses.

Essential expenses are those that are necessary for your basic needs, such as housing, food, utilities, and transportation.

Non-essential expenses are those that are not necessary for your survival, such as dining out, coffee shops, entertainment, and shopping.

After categorising your expenses, identify areas where you can cut back on spending. This could include reducing your dining out expenses, shopping at thrift stores instead of buying new clothes or cancelling subscriptions you no longer use.

Additionally, it's important to analyse any debt and create a plan to pay it off. This can include creating a debt repayment plan, prioritising debts with higher interest rates, and negotiating with creditors to reduce your interest rates. By creating a plan to pay off debt, you can reduce the amount of money you spend on interest and put more money towards your financial goals.

The Art of Setting Financial Goals

Setting financial goals is an essential part of creating a minimalist budget. Having a clear idea of your short-term and long-term financial goals will help you stay motivated and focused on your financial objectives.

Identify short-term and long-term financial goals:

Start by defining your financial goals. Short-term goals may include paying off a credit card, saving for a holiday, or building an emergency fund.

Long-term goals may include saving for retirement, buying a home, or paying off a mortgage.

Create a budget that aligns with your goals:

Once you have identified your goals, create a budget that aligns with them.

Allocate your income towards your goals, and make sure you have enough money to cover your expenses.

Track your progress and make adjustments as needed:

It is essential to track your progress towards your financial goals regularly. This will help you make adjustments to your budget as needed and keep you on track towards achieving your goals.

How to Maintain a Financial Minimalist Mindset

One of the key aspects of creating a minimalist budget is cultivating that minimalist mindset. This involves changing your approach to money and reevaluating your relationship with material possessions.

Here are some tips for sticking with a minimalist mindset after setting your financial goals and budget:

Understand the difference between needs and wants:

As discussed earlier in this chapter, it's important to differentiate between things that you need to live and things that you want. When making purchasing decisions, ask yourself if the item is a true necessity or simply a desire.

Once you can do this the next two tips become a lot easier to implement.

Practice mindful spending habits:

Before making a purchase, take a moment to consider the impact it will have on your finances. Ask yourself if the item is worth the cost and if it aligns with your financial goals. Learn to walk away if the answer is no and be honest with yourself, remember your short-term and long-term goals you set for yourself & why.

Avoid impulse purchases:

Impulse purchases can quickly add up and derail your budget. Instead, make a plan for purchases in advance and stick to it. If you see something you really want, try to give yourself a day or two to think about whether or not you really need it.

By cultivating a minimalist mindset, you can prioritise your financial goals and make intentional spending decisions that align with your values.

Minimalist Tips for Simplifying Your Budget

A. Automate your bills and savings

1. Set up automatic bill payments to avoid late fees
2. Set up automatic savings transfers to reach your financial goals faster
3. Aim to add 10% of income to savings each month

B. Use cash or debit instead of credit cards

1. Avoid interest charges and overspending
2. Stick to your budget by using only what you have left in your bank account after sending money to your savings account

C. Shop for deals and discounts

1. Look for coupons and promo codes before making purchases
2. Shop at discount stores or buy second-hand, either online or at charity shops

How to Stay Motivated and Accountable

Creating a minimalist budget is a great step towards achieving financial freedom and simplifying your life. However, staying motivated and accountable can be challenging.

Here are some tips to help you stay on track:

Create a support system:

Find a friend or family member who can hold you accountable and provide support and encouragement, someone you trust, who is willing to discuss your finances with you.

Consider joining a financial accountability group or reaching out to someone in your network who can help keep you on track.

Celebrate your financial milestones:

Take time to celebrate your accomplishments, no matter how small they may seem.

This will help you stay motivated and focused on your goals.

Continuously learn and seek advice:

Stay informed about personal finance topics and seek advice from financial experts when needed i.e. a good accountant if you are running a business or self-employed.

Attend workshops, read books and articles, and listen to podcasts to continue learning and expanding your knowledge.

By following these tips, you can stay motivated and accountable as you work towards simplifying your budget and achieving financial freedom.

Conclusion & This Week's Actionable Steps

Creating a minimalist budget can have a significant impact on your financial health and well-being.

By assessing your current financial situation, setting goals, developing a minimalist mindset, and implementing some tips for simplifying your budget, you can take control of your finances and achieve your financial goals.

To get started, **take the following action steps this week:**

1. Assess your income and expenses to gain a better understanding of your current financial situation.
2. Identify areas where you can cut back on spending and create a plan to pay off any debt.
3. Set short-term and long-term financial goals and create

a budget that aligns with those goals.
4. Automate your bills and savings, use cash or debit instead of credit cards, and simplify your investments and retirement accounts.

Remember to stay motivated and accountable by creating a support system and celebrating your financial milestones.

With these actionable steps, you can create a minimalist budget that will help you achieve financial stability, freedom and a more fulfilled lifestyle.

Week 8: Finding Work-Life Balance

Welcome to Week 8 of your minimalist journey, where we delve into the realm of simplifying your career and work life.

In this chapter, we'll explore the concept of achieving a life that's truly time-rich, where work aligns seamlessly with your passions and brings you a sense of fulfilment.

Many of us spend a substantial portion of our lives working, and it's crucial that our work contributes positively to our overall well-being.

We're going to delve into the principles of optimising your work life, finding purpose in your endeavours, and achieving satisfaction in what you do.

Whether you're navigating a traditional nine-to-five job, working a trade, pursuing freelance opportunities, or considering entrepreneurial ventures, this chapter will guide you in streamlining your work life and will help you to work towards a career that's not just about making a living but also about creating a life you truly love

Mastering the Art of a Minimalist Work-Life Balance

In our modern world, the lines between work and life can often blur, leaving us feeling overwhelmed and constantly chasing a work-life balance that seems elusive.

But what if there was a way to not only simplify your career but also transform your work-life into a source of greater freedom, purpose, and abundance?

Enter the concept of the New Rich (NR), as coined by Tim Ferris in his book The 4 Hour Work Week.

The New Rich isn't just about monetary wealth but, more importantly, about being rich in time, whether that means having more free time or just simply enjoying the time you spend working because you love what you do.

It's about breaking free from the traditional 9-to-5 grind and designing a career and work-life that aligns with your values and passions, giving you the freedom to live life on your terms.

It's a philosophy rooted in the idea that life is meant to be lived now, not postponed for some distant retirement.

Imagine a life where work is not a daily grind, but a source of passion and purpose. A life where each day is an opportunity to make a meaningful impact while still having the time to savour the simple pleasures, spend quality moments with loved ones, and explore the world.

This is what the "New Rich" work-life balance represents – a way to break free from the shackles of the conventional work week and design a life that aligns with your values and aspirations.

In exploring the concept of the "New Rich" work-life balance, it's essential to differentiate it from the traditional view of wealth.

The conventional perspective often associates richness solely with monetary affluence and the accumulation of material possessions. In this paradigm, success is measured by financial abundance and extravagant lifestyles, even if it comes at the cost of sacrificing personal time and genuine life experiences.

However, the "New Rich" offers an alternative outlook.

Take, for example, Alex, who prioritises time and experiences over material wealth. Alex lives modestly, earns a comfortable income, and channels his efforts into a life enriched by meaningful experiences, personal growth, and genuine connections.

This modern approach values a balanced, fulfilling life that extends far beyond the accumulation of money and possessions.

This week, we'll explore how to simplify your career by adopting NR principles, finding ways to increase your income, and creating the time and space for what truly matters to you. We'll discuss high-income skills, passive income streams, and how to balance your financial needs with your desire for a simpler, more fulfilling work-life.

We'll delve into the principles and practices that can help you embark on a journey toward this new way of life. We'll explore how to identify your passions, leverage your skills and resources, and carve a path that allows you to work less, live more, and ultimately find profound purpose and fulfilment in what you do.

Whether you're currently trapped in a job that doesn't align with your dreams or seeking a way to enrich your existing career, the principles of the "New Rich" work-life balance can guide you toward a brighter, more liberated future.

So, if you're ready to shift from the traditional, time-consuming career model to one that offers more freedom and flexibility, this week's minimalist challenge is your stepping stone towards becoming time-rich and embracing a career and work-life that truly enriches your life. Let's dive in!

Defining Your Ideal Work-Life Balance

To embark on a journey toward the "New Rich" work-life balance, it's essential to start by clearly defining what this balance means to you. This involves a thoughtful exploration of your values, priorities, and aspirations.

Identifying Your Values and Priorities:

Begin by reflecting on what truly matters to you. What are your core values? Is it spending more time with family, pursuing a particular passion, or simply having the freedom to explore new experiences?

By identifying your values and priorities, you'll gain a deeper understanding of what a fulfilling work-life balance looks like for you.

Assessing Your Current Work-Life Situation:

Take a close look at your current work-life situation. Are you satisfied with the way things are, or do you feel that there's room for improvement?

Consider factors such as the number of hours you dedicate to work, your level of job satisfaction, and how well your current situation aligns with your values and goals.

Setting Clear Work-Life Balance Goals:

With a clear understanding of your values and an assessment of your current situation, it's time to set concrete work-life balance goals.

These goals should be specific, measurable, and tailored to your unique aspirations.

Whether it's reducing your work hours, transitioning to a more fulfilling career, or exploring new avenues for personal growth, your goals will serve as guiding stars on your journey toward the "New Rich" work-life balance.

Defining your ideal work-life balance is a crucial first step in creating a life that aligns with your vision and values. It provides clarity and direction, helping you make intentional choices that lead to a more purposeful and time-rich existence.

Maximising Earnings and Free Time

In the pursuit of a New Rich work-life balance, it's crucial to reevaluate your approach to earning income. The traditional model of trading time for money, typically associated with the 9-to-5 job, often leaves individuals feeling time-poor and financially constrained.

The New Rich mindset, on the other hand, revolves around the concept of being time-rich, allowing you to craft a life where you're not solely reliant on a fixed job to sustain your lifestyle.

This section explores strategies for maximising earnings and creating opportunities for more free time, all while aligning with your skills, passions, and values.

Leveraging Your Skills and Passions for Income

A fundamental principle of the New Rich lifestyle is the alignment of your work with your passions and skills. Many people spend their careers in jobs that don't resonate with their interests or strengths, resulting in dissatisfaction and a sense of time slipping away.

The New Rich approach encourages you to identify your core skills and passions and explore how they can generate income.

For example, imagine you have a strong affinity for photography. Instead of viewing it as just a hobby, consider ways to turn your passion into a profitable venture.

This might involve offering photography services, selling prints, or even creating online courses to teach others. By monetising your passion, you not only boost your income but also infuse your work with purpose and fulfilment.

This alignment can significantly impact your perception of time, as the boundary between work and leisure blurs when you're engaged in something you love.

Creating Multiple Income Streams

One of the central tenets of the New Rich philosophy is diversifying your income streams.

Relying solely on a single job or income source can be financially risky and limit your freedom. To create a more resilient financial foundation and free up time, consider establishing multiple income streams.

These streams can take various forms, depending on your skills and interests. In addition to your primary job, you might explore freelance work, consulting, investments, or side businesses.

Each income stream contributes to your financial well-being, reducing the pressure to work longer hours for a single paycheck. With this diversified approach, you gain the flexibility to allocate your time more intentionally, devoting it to what matters most in your life.

Strategies for Working Smarter, Not Harder

Working smarter, not harder, is a core principle of the New Rich lifestyle. It involves optimising your work processes and prioritising tasks that yield the greatest returns, both in terms of income and time.

Here are some strategies to help you achieve this balance:

Outsourcing and Delegation:

Recognise that you don't have to do everything yourself. Delegate tasks that can be handled by others. Some of the most successful business people get to where they are purely because they have excellent delegation skills and manage people well.

Rome wasn't built in a day, it also wasn't built alone.

Doing this frees up valuable time for more meaningful activities.

Time Blocking:

Implement time-blocking techniques to structure your workday efficiently.

Set specific blocks of time for focused work, allowing you to make significant progress on important tasks without succumbing to distractions.

Leverage Technology:

Embrace technology and automation tools to streamline repetitive tasks.

Whether it's automating email responses or using project management software, these tools can save you time and mental energy.

Focus on High-Impact Tasks:

Identify tasks that have the most significant impact on your income and prioritise them.

Avoid getting bogged down by minor, low-value activities that can consume time without substantial rewards.

Set Boundaries:

Establish clear boundaries around your work hours and personal time.

Overworking may seem productive in the short term, but it can lead to burnout and a diminished quality of life. Protect your free time as sacred and vital for recharging.

Continuous Learning:

Invest in your personal and professional growth. Acquiring new skills and knowledge can open up new income opportunities and increase your earning potential.

By implementing these strategies, you can begin to shift from the traditional "time for money" model to a more flexible, efficient, and lucrative approach to work.

This transformation not only maximises your earnings but also provides you with the freedom to allocate your time where it matters most – whether that's pursuing your passions, spending time with loved ones, or simply enjoying the beauty of life.

5 Ways to Stop Exchanging Time for Money

1. Master a High-Income Skill:

Instead of trading hours for a fixed wage, focus on mastering high-income skills that allow you to charge based on the value you provide, not the time spent.

For example, becoming a digital marketing expert allows you

to offer services to clients based on the results you achieve, whether it's increasing website traffic or boosting sales. If you're more of a hands-on worker, then learning a trade or technical skill like carpentry will earn a higher income for your time.

2. Create Digital Passive Income Streams:

Invest in creating online businesses or products that generate passive income.

For instance, writing an e-book, creating an online course, or developing an app can provide ongoing revenue with minimal ongoing effort.

With effective marketing and automation, these assets can earn money while you sleep. The hard work is put in upfront, the passive income comes later.

3. Launch a Physical Product Business:

Develop a physical product that addresses a specific market need or niche. This approach allows you to sell the value of your product rather than trading time for money.

Platforms like Etsy, Amazon, Shopify, or eBay offer excellent opportunities for selling physical goods to a wide audience online.

4. Transition to an Agent Role:

If you work in a trade or any hands-on profession, consider transitioning from being a groundworker to an agent or manager.

Instead of physically doing all the work yourself, you can hire and oversee a team of skilled workers.

By taking on a managerial role, you leverage your expertise and people skills to coordinate projects, find clients, and scale your business with less time spent working in your business, and more time spent working on your business from a bird's eye view.

5. Automate and Delegate:

If you own a small business, look for opportunities to automate repetitive tasks and delegate responsibilities to employees or virtual assistants.

For example, if you run an ecommerce business you could set up automated marketing systems by hiring experts or have your products fulfilled by a fulfilment centre instead of doing this yourself.

By streamlining your business operations, you can focus on strategic decisions and expansion, reducing your direct involvement in day-to-day activities.

By adopting these strategies, you can transition away from the traditional model of exchanging time for money. Instead, you'll be on the path to financial independence and a work-life balance that aligns with your values and priorities.

Pursuing Location Independence

In today's interconnected world, achieving location independence is a goal for many seeking a New Rich work-life balance.

This section delves into strategies and considerations for embracing a lifestyle that allows you to work from anywhere while maintaining your desired income level and quality of life.

Exploring Remote Work Options:

The rise of technology has made remote work more accessible than ever.

Consider your current job, industry or skill set to determine if there are opportunities to work remotely, even on a part-time or project basis.

For those freelancing this is usually an easy step but today even those more comfortable in traditional jobs have more remote work options. Many companies now offer flexible work arrangements that allow you to complete tasks from the comfort of your home or any location with an internet connection.

Balancing Work and Travel:

One of the key advantages of location independence is the

ability to explore new places while continuing to work.

Achieving this balance requires effective time management, discipline, and a commitment to deliver results.

Research destinations with reliable Wi-Fi and consider time zones to ensure that your work hours align with your clients or employer.

Embracing the Freedom to Work from Anywhere:

Once you've secured location-independent work, you'll have the freedom to choose where you live and how you allocate your time.

Whether you dream of working by a tropical beach, a bustling city, or a serene mountain retreat, the possibilities are endless when working remotely.

Deciding on Location Independence in Your Career or Business Path:

Before embarking on a journey towards location independence, take time to reflect on whether this lifestyle aligns with your career or business goals.

For some, being tethered to a specific location is integral to their profession or passion, while others thrive in roles that offer geographical flexibility.

Consider your priorities, values, and long-term vision to

determine whether location independence is a key component of your desired work-life balance.

Achieving location independence is a journey that allows you to break free from the constraints of a traditional office and experience the world on your terms. It opens doors to new adventures, cultures, and opportunities while maintaining financial stability.

In the pursuit of a New Rich work-life balance, location independence is a powerful avenue to explore.

Crafting a Purposeful Work-Life

Creating a work-life balance extends beyond financial considerations; it's about finding meaning and fulfilment in your career.

This section explores the process of crafting a purposeful work life that aligns with your values, strengths, and passions.

Finding Meaning and Fulfilment in Your Career:

Many people spend a significant portion of their lives working, making it crucial to find purpose and satisfaction in what you do.

Reflect on your current job or career path to identify aspects that resonate with your values and bring a sense of fulfilment.

Consider the impact your work has on others and the world at large. Seek opportunities to contribute positively and align your efforts with a greater purpose and if you do not see any of these things currently then it could be a sign it's time to consider changing your path.

Identifying Your Unique Strengths and Talents:

To create a purposeful work life, it's essential to recognise your unique strengths and talents.

What are you exceptionally good at? What tasks or activities bring you joy and energise you?

Conduct self-assessments, seek feedback from peers and mentors, and explore your interests to gain clarity on your strengths.

Leveraging these strengths in your career can help you make a stronger impact and lead to a more purposeful and fulfilling work experience.

Aligning Your Work with Your Life Purpose:

Crafting a purposeful work life often involves aligning your career with your life purpose.

Your life purpose represents the overarching mission or calling that guides your choices and actions. It can encompass personal values, passions, and the positive impact you want to make on the world.

Explore how you would like your current job or business endeavours to align with your life purpose, and identify areas where adjustments or changes may be needed to achieve a greater sense of purpose.

Achieving a positive work-life balance includes the pursuit of a career that not only sustains you financially but also fuels your sense of purpose and fulfilment.

By finding meaning in your work, leveraging your strengths, and aligning your career with your life purpose, you can embark on a journey toward a work-life balance that enriches your overall well-being.

Simplifying Your Workday

Creating a better work-life balance involves simplifying your workday to make the most of your time and optimise productivity.

In this section, we'll explore strategies for streamlining tasks, minimising distractions, and managing your time effectively.

Streamlining Tasks and Responsibilities:

Start by evaluating your daily tasks and responsibilities.

Identify areas where you can streamline processes, automate repetitive tasks, or delegate assignments when possible.

Simplify your workload by focusing on high-impact activities that align with your career goals and priorities.

Eliminate tasks that do not contribute significantly to your work's overall value.

Minimising Distractions and Interruptions:

Distractions and interruptions can significantly impact your productivity. Take proactive steps to minimise these disruptions.

Designate specific time blocks for focused work, and communicate your need for uninterrupted work periods to colleagues or family members.

Silence unnecessary notifications on your devices and create a distraction-free workspace.

Consider implementing techniques like the Pomodoro method, which involves short, focused work sessions followed by brief breaks.

Use the Pomodoro Technique to Increase Focus:

The Pomodoro Technique is a time management method developed by Francesco Cirillo in the late 1980s.

It's designed to improve productivity and focus by breaking work into intervals, traditionally 25 minutes in length, separated by short breaks. These intervals are often referred to as

"Pomodoros."

During each Pomodoro, you commit to working on a single task or project with intense concentration. When the timer rings, you take a short break of around 5 minutes to relax, stretch, or clear your mind. After completing four Pomodoros, you take a longer break of 15-30 minutes.

The Pomodoro Technique helps individuals maintain focus and avoid burnout by breaking work into manageable chunks. It encourages a sense of urgency during the 25-minute intervals while allowing brief respites to recharge.

Many people find it an effective way to combat procrastination and boost productivity in both professional and personal tasks.

You can also edit the time frames used to suit your work style better if needed.

Time Management Techniques for Increased Productivity:

Effective time management is a key component of a purposeful work life. Explore time management techniques such as the Eisenhower Matrix for prioritizing tasks and getting more done.

Research and use digital tools, such as task management apps and calendars, to stay organised and track your progress. Use the tools you find that you feel work best for your work style.

The Eisenhower Matrix: A Tool for Effective Task Prioritiza-

tion:

The Eisenhower Matrix, also known as the Urgent-Important Matrix, is a powerful tool for organising tasks and determining their priority.

The matrix divides tasks into four distinct categories:

Urgent and Important (Quadrant I):

Tasks in this category are both urgent and essential. They require immediate attention because they have a significant impact on your goals, well-being, or work.

These are your top priorities, and they should be addressed promptly. Examples of tasks in this quadrant include meeting deadlines, dealing with emergencies, and handling critical work assignments.

Important but Not Urgent (Quadrant II):

This quadrant focuses on tasks that are essential but do not require immediate action. They contribute to your long-term goals, personal development, and overall well-being.

To make the most of your time, it's crucial to schedule these tasks and allocate dedicated time for them. Examples include strategic planning, skill development, and maintaining healthy relationships.

Urgent but Not Important (Quadrant III):

Tasks in this quadrant are often deceptive because they feel urgent but do not contribute significantly to your goals or well-being. They are often distractions that can consume your time and energy.

It's essential to minimise or delegate these tasks whenever possible. Examples include unnecessary meetings, interruptions, and unimportant emails.

Neither Urgent nor Important (Quadrant IV):

Tasks in this quadrant are neither urgent nor important. They are time-wasters that provide little to no value. It's best to avoid, limit or eliminate these tasks altogether.

Examples include mindless scrolling on social media, excessive TV watching, or attending events that you would rather not be at.

Using the Eisenhower Matrix can help you:

- Prioritise tasks effectively by separating the urgent from the non-urgent and the important from the less important.
- Allocate your time and energy efficiently to tasks that align with your goals and values.
- Reduce stress by addressing critical matters promptly and proactively planning for important but non-urgent tasks.
- Make informed decisions about what tasks to focus on, delegate, or eliminate.

Achieving a good work-life balance requires simplifying your workday to get more done in the hours designated to work, and creating more time in the day for rest or other activities that matter to you.

By streamlining tasks and responsibilities, minimising distractions, and mastering time management techniques, you can boost productivity, reduce stress, and enhance your overall work-life satisfaction.

Achieving Work-Life Harmony: Balancing Your Priorities

In the pursuit of a meaningful and fulfilling life, achieving work-life harmony plays a pivotal role.

It's not just about managing time; it's about aligning your priorities, values, and responsibilities to create a sense of balance and fulfilment.

Balancing Work, Family, and Personal Time:

Striking a balance between your professional life, family commitments, and personal time is a perpetual challenge.

To achieve work-life harmony, start by clearly defining your priorities. Identify the essential aspects of your life, including your career, relationships, health, and personal growth.

Allocate time and energy to each of these areas based on their importance. Establish boundaries to protect your personal and family time, ensuring that work doesn't encroach on these crucial moments.

Learn to Say No to Being Overwhelmed:

In our fast-paced world, it's easy to fall into the trap of overcommitting and feeling overwhelmed.

Learning to say no is a valuable skill.

Evaluate new requests, opportunities, or responsibilities carefully. Consider whether they align with your goals and values and whether you have the capacity to take them on without compromising your well-being.

Saying no when necessary allows you to focus on your existing commitments and maintain a healthy work-life balance.

Cultivating a Rich and Balanced Life:

Work-life harmony extends beyond the absence of stress; it's about leading a rich and fulfilling life.

Cultivate hobbies, interests, and activities that bring joy and purpose to your days.

Invest time in self-care practices that support your physical and mental well-being.

Prioritise quality time with loved ones and build meaningful connections.

Remember that work is just one facet of your life; nurturing other aspects enhances your overall satisfaction and sense of fulfilment.

Work-life harmony isn't a one-size-fits-all concept. It's a dynamic and evolving process that requires self-awareness, adaptability, and conscious decision-making. Regularly assess your priorities, adjust your commitments as needed, and ensure that your daily choices align with your overarching goals for a balanced and meaningful life.

By implementing these strategies and maintaining a focus on your well-being, relationships, and personal growth, you can cultivate a harmonious life that resonates with your values and aspirations.

Work should complement your life, not overshadow it, and achieving that harmony is a journey well worth taking.

Conclusion and Actionable Steps for Achieving a Balanced Work-Life

In concluding this chapter on achieving a balanced work life, it's important to reiterate the significance of aligning your professional endeavours with your personal aspirations.

The principles of minimalist work-life balance emphasise the value of time, purpose, and fulfilment in crafting a meaningful existence.

Let's summarise these key principles and outline actionable steps to help you embark on your journey towards a harmonious and purposeful work-life.

Key Principles for a Minimalist Work-Life Balance:

Prioritise Your Values: Identify your core values and priorities, both in your career and personal life. Use these as guiding principles to make decisions that resonate with your authentic self.

Say No When Necessary: Learn to say no to commitments, tasks, or responsibilities that don't align with your goals or values. Saying no allows you to protect your time and maintain balance.

Cultivate Balance: Allocate time to various life domains, including work, family, health, and personal growth. Maintain boundaries to safeguard your personal and family time.

Nurture a Fully Rich Life: Beyond work, cultivate hobbies, interests, and relationships that bring joy and purpose to your life. Self-care and meaningful connections contribute to overall well-being.

Work Efficiently: Implement time management techniques, such as the Pomodoro method and the Eisenhower Matrix, to block important tasks, boost productivity and reduce stress.

Actionable Steps for Achieving a Balanced Work Life:

1. Define Your Priorities & Purpose:

Take some time to reflect on your core values and priorities in both your career and personal life.

What truly matters to you? Write down your top three values or priorities.

This exercise will help you gain clarity on what you want to focus on.

2. Create a Weekly Schedule:

Craft a weekly schedule that reflects your priorities. Allocate dedicated time to each of your top values or priorities.

Ensure there's a healthy balance between work, family, self-care, and personal interests in your schedule.

3. Time Management Experiment:

Experiment with a time management technique that resonates with you. It could be the Pomodoro method, the Eisenhower Matrix, or another method you've discovered.

Apply this technique to a specific task or project this week and assess its impact on your productivity and work-life balance.

4. Time Audit and Adjustment:

Conduct a thorough time audit of your typical workday.

Identify areas where you might be spending too much time on low-value tasks or distractions.

Then, make a conscious effort to adjust your daily routine to allocate more time to tasks that align with your priorities and values, ensuring a more balanced work-life harmony.

5. Craft a Purposeful Work-Life:

Reflect on your career and life goals. Consider whether your current job or business aligns with your life's mission and values.

If not, create a work-life plan that enables you to transition into a more meaningful job, learn high-income skills, or develop a passive income business that provides greater satisfaction and fulfilment.

6. Assess Financial Opportunities:

Review your financial situation and last week's exercise on budget simplification. Assess whether further cost-cutting measures can help you create a better work-life balance.

By reducing unnecessary expenses, you may find the freedom to work less, explore more meaningful career options, or dedicate time to your personal growth and well-being.

These actionable steps will further support your journey toward a balanced work life, focusing on building meaningful connections, optimising your time, aligning your career with your purpose, and ensuring your financial situation supports your desired work-life harmony.

Remember that continuous self-assessment and adaptation are key to maintaining this balance in the long term.

Week 9: Embracing Slow Living

Live More by Doing Less

In today's fast-paced world, it can be challenging to find moments of peace and relaxation.

We often prioritise our work and other responsibilities, leaving little time for ourselves.

By embracing slow living, we can improve our well-being and find a sense of fulfilment in our daily lives.

In this chapter, we will explore what slow living means and the benefits of adopting this lifestyle. We will also discuss practical ways to incorporate slow living into our lives.

Slow living is not just a lifestyle but a state of mind. It is a way of living intentionally and mindfully, with the goal of finding peace and contentment in the present moment.

The principles of slow living align with many of the topics

covered in previous weeks.

For instance, setting a minimalist budget is a way to simplify your finances and reduce stress. Detaching from material possessions helps you focus on what truly matters, such as relationships and experiences.

Cooking healthy meals is a way to nourish your body and appreciate the process of creating something from scratch.

Finding joy in simple things, such as spending time in nature, reading a book, or listening to music, is a way to cultivate gratitude and mindfulness in your daily life.

By embracing slow living, you can learn to appreciate the present moment, live more intentionally, and find contentment in a slower pace of life.

Slow living has its roots in various philosophical and spiritual traditions, including Taoism, Stoicism, and Zen.

These traditions emphasise the importance of living in the present moment, cultivating mindfulness, and simplifying one's life in order to attain a deeper sense of contentment and fulfilment.

In Taoism, the concept of wu wei, or "non-doing," encourages individuals to let go of the need to control every aspect of their lives and instead embrace the natural flow of things.

This involves slowing down and being more present in the

moment, rather than rushing through life in a constant state of busyness and distraction.

Similarly, the Stoics believed in the importance of living in harmony with nature and accepting things as they are, rather than striving for constant growth and progress.

This mindset is reflected in the Stoic principle of "amor fati," which means "love of fate" and encourages individuals to embrace whatever happens in their lives as an opportunity for growth and learning.

In Zen, the practice of mindfulness meditation and the concept of "mushin," or "no-mind," emphasise the importance of living in the present moment and letting go of attachment to thoughts, emotions, and material possessions.

This allows individuals to cultivate a sense of inner peace and clarity, which can help them navigate life's challenges with greater ease and grace.

These philosophical traditions provide a rich framework for understanding the principles of slow living and offer valuable insights into the benefits of simplifying one's life, embracing mindfulness, and cultivating a deeper sense of contentment and fulfilment.

Evaluating Your Current Pace of Life

Evaluating your current pace of life is an essential first step in embracing slow living. It involves taking a step back and reflecting on how you currently spend your time and energy.

One effective approach is to examine your priorities and values and determine if they align with your current lifestyle.

Ask yourself what truly matters to you and what brings you joy and fulfilment?

Are you spending enough time on those things, or are you constantly rushing from one obligation to another without taking a moment to appreciate the present moment?

Identifying areas where you can slow down is another important aspect of evaluating your current pace of life.

This could involve cutting back on certain activities or commitments that are draining your energy and causing unnecessary stress. It could also involve creating more space in your schedule for relaxation and self-care activities, such as meditation, yoga, or spending time in nature.

Recognising the signs of burnout is also crucial in evaluating your current pace of life.

Burnout is a state of physical, emotional, and mental exhaustion that results from chronic stress and overworking.

It can manifest as fatigue, irritability, anxiety, and a lack of motivation.

If you are experiencing any of these symptoms, it may be a sign that you need to slow down and take a break.

This could involve taking a day off from work, scheduling a weekend getaway, or simply saying no to certain commitments that are causing you undue stress.

By taking proactive steps to avoid burnout, you can maintain your health and well-being and prevent long-term damage to your mental and physical health.

The Zen saying *"If you don't have time to meditate for an hour, you should meditate for two hours"* highlights the importance of slowing down and taking time for self-care practices, even when our schedules are busy.

In the context of slow living, this quote reminds us that it's often when we feel the most pressed for time that we need to take a step back and intentionally slow down.

By prioritising activities like meditation or mindfulness, we can cultivate a greater sense of presence and awareness in our daily lives, allowing us to appreciate the simple joys of living and reducing feelings of overwhelm and burnout.

Understanding your priorities and values

Understanding your priorities and values is a crucial step

towards living a minimalist and fulfilling life.

Minimalism is the intentional choice to live with less, focusing on what truly matters and eliminating not only possessions but also distractions that do not add value to your life.

By identifying your priorities and values, you can focus on what truly matters to you and eliminate the excess that may be weighing you down.

For example, if your priority is to spend more time with your family, you may choose to simplify your schedule and reduce the number of commitments that take you away from home.

In the same way, by living a minimalist lifestyle, you can reduce the clutter and noise in your life, freeing up space and time for the things that matter most to you. This may include simplifying your home, reducing your possessions, and minimising your expenses.

Living a minimalist and fulfilling life requires discipline, intentionality, and a commitment to your values. It means being intentional about your choices, focusing on what brings you joy and purpose, and letting go of the excess that does not align with your priorities.

In summary, understanding your priorities and values is an essential aspect of living a minimalist and fulfilling life.

By identifying what truly matters to you and eliminating distractions, you can focus on the things that bring you joy, purpose, and fulfilment, leading to a simpler, more intentional, and more fulfilling life

Identifying Areas Where You Can Slow Down

Identifying areas where you can slow down is an important step towards living a more intentional and fulfilling life.

In today's fast-paced world, it's easy to get caught up in the hustle and bustle of daily life, which can leave us feeling stressed, overwhelmed, and disconnected.

Slowing down means intentionally taking a step back from the rush of daily life to reflect, recharge, and focus on what truly matters.

This may involve reducing the pace of your work or personal life, saying "no" to unnecessary commitments, or taking more time for self-care and relaxation.

To identify areas where you can slow down, start by assessing your current lifestyle and identifying areas that feel particularly hectic or stressful. This may include work, social commitments, household chores, or even hobbies and leisure activities.

Once you have identified the areas that feel overwhelming, consider ways to simplify or streamline them.

This may involve delegating tasks, reducing your workload, altering your schedule to allow more time to do those tasks you are overwhelmed by, or setting boundaries with others to ensure that your time and energy are being used in the most meaningful and fulfilling ways.

Slowing down also means taking time to reflect and recharge.

This may involve setting aside time for meditation, journaling, or other mindfulness practices that help you connect with yourself and your values.

here are some additional tips on how to slow down and still maintain a clean and organised home:

Prioritise:

Take a moment to assess which household chores are essential and which ones can wait. Prioritising tasks can help you focus on the most important tasks and reduce the stress and overwhelm of trying to do everything at once.

Break tasks into smaller pieces:

Instead of tackling a big cleaning project all at once, try breaking it down into smaller, manageable tasks. This can make the work feel less daunting and more achievable.

Set a timer:

When you're feeling overwhelmed by household chores, try setting a timer for a specific amount of time, like 15 or 30 minutes. During that time, focus solely on the task at hand

and see how much progress you can make. Once the timer goes off, take a break and come back to it later.

Make it enjoyable:

Try to find ways to make household chores more enjoyable. You could listen to your favourite music or podcast while you clean, or use your favourite cleaning supplies that have a pleasant scent.

Involve others:

If you have family members or roommates, consider involving them in the cleaning process. This can help lighten the load plus make the work feel more of a team effort and less overwhelming.

Simplify:

If you find that certain household chores are taking up too much time and energy, consider simplifying the task. For example, you could reduce the number of dishes you use by using the same plate for multiple meals or reduce the amount of clutter in your home by regularly donating or selling items you no longer need.

Remember, the goal of slowing down is to reduce stress and overwhelm, so it's important to find a pace that works for you.

By taking a step back, prioritising tasks, and finding ways to make household chores more enjoyable, you can still maintain a clean and organised home without feeling like you're constantly rushing.

Try to focus on the satisfaction and pleasant feelings you get and adopt a more mindful approach to household tasks. Start to visualise them more as mindful activities you carry out, rather than seeing them as chores that you dread doing.

Find peace in the moment of the activity you are carrying out, put all your focus into it and try to stop worrying about external things that aren't anything to do with what you are doing right in that moment.

Identifying areas where you can slow down is an important step towards living a more intentional and fulfilling life.

By intentionally reducing the pace of your daily life, you can focus on what truly matters, reduce stress and overwhelm, and create more space for the things that bring you joy and fulfilment.

Recognising the signs of burnout

Recognising the signs of burnout is essential to maintaining your well-being and preventing long-term negative effects.

Burnout is a state of emotional, physical, and mental exhaustion that can be caused by prolonged periods of stress and overworking.

Common signs of burnout include chronic fatigue, irritability, cynicism, and a lack of motivation or engagement in work or other activities.

Other signs may include physical symptoms such as headaches, digestive issues, and muscle tension.

If you are experiencing any of these signs, it's important to take steps to address them.

This may include taking a break, seeking support from loved ones or a professional, and reassessing your priorities and boundaries. Recognising and addressing burnout can help you regain a sense of balance and prevent further negative impacts on your well-being.

One way to recognise and address the cause of burnout is to examine your lifestyle and determine if you are living in alignment with your values and priorities.

As we previously discussed, slowing down can help you reflect on what truly matters and identify areas where you can simplify or streamline your life.

By reassessing your priorities and boundaries, you may be able to identify areas where you are overworking or overstressing yourself and take steps to address them.

For example, you may find that you are spending too much time on work or social commitments that don't align with your values, leaving you feeling drained and unfulfilled.

By slowing down and reflecting on what matters most to you, you may be able to restructure your schedule or say "no" to certain commitments to create more space for the things that bring you joy and fulfilment. This can help reduce stress and prevent burnout in the long term.

Another important aspect of addressing burnout and living a slower, more fulfilling life is to avoid being too hard on yourself or expecting to achieve too much at once.

As we discussed earlier, slowing down requires a shift in mindset and expectations. It's important to treat life as a marathon, not a sprint, and to give yourself permission to rest and recharge as needed.

By taking a gentler approach to life and focusing on small, achievable goals, you can reduce stress and overwhelm and prevent burnout.

Remember, the goal of slowing down is not perfection but rather progress and growth.

Celebrate your small wins along the way and don't be too hard on yourself if you slip up or make mistakes.

By practising self-compassion and treating yourself with kindness and understanding, you can create a more enjoyable, peaceful and fulfilling life.

Implementing Slow Living Practices

In order to embrace slow living, it is a good idea to implement practices that align with a slower pace of life.

This includes practices such as mindfulness, simplifying your schedule, and taking time for rest and relaxation.

By engaging in these practices, you can find greater fulfilment and joy in your daily life while avoiding burnout and overwhelm.

In this section, we will discuss some practical ways to implement slow-living practices into your daily routine.

Practising Mindfulness and Being in the Present Moment:

"Be here now." - Ram Dass

Practising mindfulness involves focusing on the present moment and getting lost in the task at hand rather than worrying about external problems or all the other things you have to do.

It's about fully submerging yourself in every action you carry out, whether it's washing dishes, walking to work, or folding laundry.

Mindfulness can be incorporated into daily activities, such as mindful walking or breathing exercises, to help you cultivate a deeper sense of awareness and appreciation for the present moment.

By practising mindfulness, you can learn to let go of distractions and be fully present in your daily life.

Practising mindfulness and being present in the moment is an essential aspect of slow living.

One way to incorporate mindfulness into your daily routine is by practising mindful walking. Instead of rushing through your commute or walking to complete a task, take the time to focus on the sensations in your body and the environment around you. Notice the sights, sounds, and smells, and how they make you feel.

Another way to practice mindfulness is by incorporating mindful breathing exercises into your daily routine. Taking deep breaths can help you slow down, reduce stress, and increase your sense of calm.

By intentionally slowing down and being fully present in each moment, you can bring a sense of mindfulness to all your daily activities, from preparing a meal to spending time with loved ones.

> "Most humans are never fully present in the now, because unconsciously they believe that the next moment must be more important than this one. But

then you miss your whole life, which is never not now." - *Eckhart Tolle*

Taking time for rest and relaxation:

In today's fast-paced world, many of us are constantly caught up in a cycle of doing, achieving, and striving.

We believe that our worth is defined by our productivity and that taking a break is a sign of weakness. But this way of living is not sustainable, and it can lead to burnout, anxiety, and a sense of disconnection from ourselves and the world around us.

As discussed in the previous chapter **taking regular breaks** is actually key to **getting more done** with time-blocking techniques such as the Pomodoro technique.

To truly embrace slow living, we must learn to prioritise rest and relaxation. This means carving out time in our busy schedules for activities that nourish our bodies and souls, such as meditation, yoga, stretching, exercising, reading, or spending time in nature.

In these moments of stillness, we have the opportunity to connect with our inner selves and cultivate a sense of inner peace.

We can let go of our worries and concerns, and simply be present in the moment. By taking the time to rest and recharge, we are able to approach our work and responsibilities with renewed energy and clarity.

Remember that rest is not a luxury, but a necessity.

It is not something to be earned or deserved, but a fundamental part of our being. So the next time you feel the urge to push through exhaustion or burnout, take a step back and give yourself permission to rest, even if that just means a short break to get up, go to the kitchen and get a glass of water, a small break can make a world of difference.

Engaging in activities that bring joy and fulfilment

To engage in activities that bring joy and fulfilment is to live in alignment with your true purpose.

These activities do not have to be grand or ambitious. They can be as simple as taking a walk in nature, reading a book, or spending time with loved ones.

The key is to approach these activities with a sense of presence and awareness, allowing yourself to fully enjoy the experience without worrying about the past or the future.

Embrace the power of stillness and allow yourself to be fully present in the moment.

By focusing on activities that bring joy and fulfilment, you begin to cultivate a sense of gratitude and contentment in your life.

You learn to appreciate the simple things and find beauty in the ordinary. This helps to shift your perspective from one of lack and scarcity to one of abundance and possibility.

So take the time to identify the activities that truly bring you joy and make them a priority in your life.

Whether it's painting, gardening, or playing an instrument, these activities can help you connect with your true self and find a sense of peace and fulfilment in the present moment.

Here's a list of some ideas for inspiration and examples

1. Spending time in nature
2. Practising a creative hobby, such as painting or writing
3. Listening to music or attending a concert
4. Trying new foods or cooking a favourite dish
5. Reading a good book
6. Volunteering for a cause you believe in
7. Travelling to a new place or revisiting a favourite destination
8. Practising yoga or another form of physical exercise
9. Having meaningful conversations with loved ones
10. Going to a museum or art exhibit
11. Watching a movie or TV show that inspires you
12. Learning a new skill or taking a class
13. Spending time with pets or animals
14. Doing something adventurous, like hiking or skydiving
15. Going to a spa or taking a relaxing bath
16. Participating in a spiritual or religious practice
17. Connecting with your community through social events

or gatherings
18. Practising meditation
19. Attending a lecture or workshop on a topic you're interested in
20. Engaging in any hobby or activity that challenges you and helps you grow.

Finding Community and Support

One of the keys to living a slow and mindful life is surrounding yourself with like-minded individuals who share your values and goals.

Surrounding yourself with like-minded individuals can be an essential step towards embracing slow living.

It's important to connect with others who share similar values and priorities to maintain a sense of community and mutual support.

This can include joining local groups or clubs that align with your interests, attending workshops or events centred around mindfulness or slow-living activities such as cooking classes, or simply reaching out to friends and family members who also prioritise a slower, more intentional lifestyle.

In addition to finding community, building a support system can also provide accountability and encouragement on your slow-living journey.

This can include sharing your goals and progress with trusted friends or family members, participating in support groups or online forums, or even hiring a coach or therapist who specialises in slow living and mindfulness practices.

Having a support system can help keep you motivated and accountable, as well as provide valuable insights and feedback as you navigate the challenges and rewards of living a slower, more intentional life.

Joining a yoga class or a meditation group, for example, can be a great way to connect with others who are also interested in mindfulness and living a slower, more intentional life.

Other ways to find community and support include joining a book club, volunteering for a local organisation, or attending a workshop or retreat focused on slow living or mindfulness.

These types of activities not only provide opportunities to connect with others but also allow you to learn new skills and gain fresh perspectives on how to live a more fulfilling life.

Staying Committed to Slow Living

Slow living is not a one-time event; it requires a commitment to a lifestyle that may be challenging at times.

It is normal to face setbacks and difficulties, such as feeling overwhelmed or getting caught up in the fast-paced culture of our modern society.

When this happens, it is important to remember why you started and to refocus your attention on your priorities and values. Overcoming these challenges will allow you to fully embrace the benefits of slow living.

Continuing to prioritise slow living practices is key to sustaining this lifestyle. It should be helpful having a routine that includes specific activities such as daily meditation or a regular walk in nature (as discussed in previous chapters).

By making these practices a part of your routine, it becomes easier to incorporate them into your daily life. It is also important to remain mindful of your priorities and values, ensuring that your actions align with your intentions.

Finally, celebrating progress and accomplishments is an important aspect of staying committed to slow living. Take time to acknowledge your achievements and reflect on how far you have come.

Celebrate small milestones and use them as motivation to continue making progress towards your goals. By recognising and celebrating your progress, you can stay motivated and committed to living a slow and intentional life.

Conclusion & Your Actionable Steps for Week 7

Now that you have learned about the benefits of slow living and ways to implement it into your life, it's time to take action.

WEEK 9: EMBRACING SLOW LIVING

Start by evaluating your current pace of life and identifying areas where you can slow down.

Then, practice mindfulness and being present in every moment, finding joy in simple activities, and taking time for rest and relaxation.

It's also important to find like-minded individuals and build a support system for accountability and encouragement.

Joining a yoga class or meditation group, volunteering in your community, or attending local events are great ways to connect with others who share similar values.

Remember that staying committed to slow living may come with challenges and setbacks, but it's important to continue prioritising these practices.

Celebrate your progress and accomplishments along the way, and don't forget to regularly evaluate and adjust your habits to ensure they align with your values and priorities.

This week make time to do each of these easy tasks:

- Focus on being present in the moment, especially during daily activities - try to still your mind from worrying about the past or future and just focus on the present.

- Identify areas where you can cut back and make time for

relaxation and self-care.

- Find one way to connect with like-minded people; such as joining a yoga class, meditation group, volunteer group, cooking class, book club, reaching out to a friend who shares the same values or attending local events that embrace slow living activities.

In summary, slow living can bring many benefits to your life, including increased mindfulness, reduced stress, and a greater appreciation for the present moment.

By implementing slow living practices and finding community and support, you can create a more intentional and fulfilling lifestyle.

So take action this week and continue making positive changes for your well-being and happiness.

Week 10: Crafting A Minimalist Exercise Routine

In the pursuit of a simpler and more mindful life, one facet that should never be overlooked is the profound impact of exercise on our overall well-being.

Exercise is not just a means to sculpt our bodies; it's a path to nurturing our minds and spirits as well.

In this weeks chapter, we'll delve into the realm of minimalist exercise—a holistic approach to staying active that seamlessly integrates with your unique goals and the rhythm of your life.

The beauty of minimalist exercise lies in its versatility. Unlike rigid, one-size-fits-all fitness routines, this approach adapts to your individual goals and schedules.

Whether you're striving for weight loss, muscle gain, stress reduction, or enhanced flexibility, minimalist exercise can be customised to meet your needs. The key lies in its simplicity and consistency—principles that align perfectly with the minimalist lifestyle we've been cultivating throughout this journey.

Simplicity, in this context, means that you don't need a vast array of gym equipment or complex routines to achieve your fitness objectives.

Minimalist exercise is about stripping away the unnecessary and focusing on what truly matters. It's an invitation to let go of the noise and clutter that often accompany modern fitness trends, replacing them with straightforward, effective, and enjoyable practices.

Consistency, on the other hand, is the heartbeat of any successful fitness regimen. By integrating exercise seamlessly into your daily life, you'll build a foundation of wellness that can be sustained over the long term.

Minimalist exercise isn't about extreme workouts that leave you exhausted; it's about crafting a sustainable routine that brings you joy and vitality each day.

As we explore the world of mindful movement and minimalist exercise, keep in mind that your fitness journey is a deeply personal one. It's about nurturing your physical health, calming your mind, and nurturing your spirit. It's about discovering what makes you feel vibrant and alive.

So, let's embark on this chapter with an open mind and heart with a sense of curiosity, knowing that through simplicity and consistency, we can create a fitness routine that harmonises perfectly with our minimalist lifestyles.

Defining Your Fitness Goals

In your minimalist exercise journey, it's essential to begin with a clear sense of purpose.

Defining your fitness goals not only provides direction but also serves as your motivating force. Exercise becomes more meaningful when it aligns with your aspirations and desires.

Fitness goals come in various forms, reflecting your unique priorities and interests. Here are some examples to consider:

1. Weight Loss:

- If shedding extra pounds and improving your overall health are your primary aims, then your fitness journey might revolve around calorie-burning activities like jogging, cycling, or swimming. High-intensity interval training (HIIT) and bodyweight exercises can also be powerful allies in your weight loss quest.

2. Muscle Gain:

- For those looking to build lean muscle mass, resistance training exercises such as weightlifting, calisthenics, or yoga can be particularly effective. These activities help you sculpt your physique while enhancing strength and flexibility.

3. Mental Well Being:

- Physical activity is a powerful tool for stress management and mental health. Yoga, tai chi, and mindful walking are excellent choices for reducing stress and promoting relaxation. Engaging in any form of regular exercise releases endorphins, which are natural mood lifters. Even activities that might not generally be associated specifically with mindfulness such as team sports, running, weight lifting or dancing can all take you into the present moment and induce a state of flow, having a profound impact on reducing stress, anxiety, and depression while enhancing overall mental clarity.

4. Flexibility:

- If your goal is to enhance your flexibility and mobility, practices like yoga, Pilates, or dedicated stretching routines can work wonders. These exercises promote joint health, prevent injuries, and increase overall suppleness.

Now, as you embark on this chapter, I encourage you to identify your specific objectives.

What are you striving to achieve through exercise?

Consider what truly resonates with you and aligns with your minimalist lifestyle. It might be a combination of these goals, and that's perfectly fine. Your fitness journey is a personal voyage, and you have the liberty to tailor it to your unique desires and needs.

Remember that minimalist exercise isn't confined to the walls of a gym or running on a treadmill.

Your fitness routine can encompass a wide array of activities and formats. From calisthenics that can be done anywhere with little to no equipment, leveraging your body weight for resistance, to joining sports clubs or teams that participate in your favourite sports—there are countless ways to craft a fitness regimen that feels inspiring and fulfilling to you.

As you progress through this chapter, keep your fitness goals at the forefront of your mind. They will serve as your compass, guiding you toward a minimalist exercise routine that aligns seamlessly with your life.

If you are not interested in team sports or exercising solely to keep fit then maybe there's something else out there for you that you could find fun. Consider these options below if you need something new to get you inspired and excited to exercise:

- 1. Mountain Biking: Conquer off-road trails and work on endurance and balance.
- 2. Cycling: Take scenic rides on your bike to improve cardiovascular health.
- 3. Skateboarding: Master tricks and balance while cruising on your skateboard.
- 4. Surfing: Catch waves and enhance core strength and balance.
- 5. Snowboarding: Navigate down snow-covered slopes for an adrenaline rush.
- 6. Skiing: Glide on snowy terrains, working on your agility

and control.
- 7. Artistic Skating: Express creativity through dances and graceful moves on rollerskates.
- 8. Dancing: Join dance classes to learn various styles and boost cardiovascular fitness.
- 9. Ice Skating: Glide gracefully on ice rinks while enhancing lower body strength.
- 10. Calisthenics: Build strength and flexibility through bodyweight exercises.
- 11. Jam Skating: Dance on wheels while improving leg strength and coordination.
- 12. Gymnastics: Develop flexibility, balance, and body control with gymnastic routines.
- 13. Parkour: Master efficient movement and agility as you navigate obstacles.
- 14. Hiking: Explore natural landscapes while improving stamina and leg strength.
- 15. Rock Climbing: Scale indoor or outdoor climbing walls for upper body strength.
- 16. Yoga: Cultivate mindfulness, flexibility, and balance through yoga practice.
- 17. Pilates: Strengthen your core muscles and improve posture with Pilates.
- 18. Martial Arts: Learn self-defence while enhancing discipline and fitness.
- 19. Ultimate Frisbee: Participate in a dynamic team sport for cardio and agility.
- 20. Rowing: Get on the water or use a rowing machine to boost full-body strength.
- 21. Aerial Arts: Experiment with aerial silks, hoops, or pole dancing for upper body and core strength.

- 22. Synchronized Swimming: Combine swimming with dance and coordination.
- 23. Ballet: Embrace the elegance of ballet while improving flexibility and balance.
- 24. Trampoline: Bounce on trampolines for fun cardiovascular exercise.
- 25. Circus Arts: Try your hand at juggling, clowning, or acrobatics for diverse skills.
- 26. Fencing: Engage in duels while honing agility and mental focus.
- 27. Kickboxing: Blend martial arts and boxing for an intense workout.
- 28. Mountain Climbing: Ascend natural peaks while building mental and physical resilience.
- 29. Sailing: Navigate waters while learning wind control and teamwork.
- 30. Synchronized Skating: Skate in formations with a team for a creative experience.
- 31. Racquet Sports: Enjoy tennis, badminton, paddle tennis, squash, table tennis or pickleball for social and active fun.
- 32. Paddleboarding: Explore waterways while balancing on a stand-up paddleboard.
- 33. Aerial Silks: Learn graceful movements and build strength while suspended from fabric.
- 34. Capoeira: Experience the Brazilian martial art that combines elements of dance and acrobatics.
- 35. Trail Running: Add excitement to your running routine by hitting the trails.
- 36. Stand-Up Paddleboard Yoga: Combine balance and mindfulness on a paddleboard.

- 37. Slacklining: Enhance your balance and concentration on a slackline.
- 38. Kiteboarding: Harness the wind to glide across the water with a kiteboard.
- 39. Swimming: Dive into a low-impact, full-body workout in the pool.
- 40. Athletics: Engage in running, jumping, throwing, and other track and field events to test your speed, strength, and agility.

Crafting Your Minimalist Exercise Plan

Alright, let's dive into the nitty-gritty of crafting your very own minimalist exercise plan. No need for complicated fitness jargon or overwhelming routines; we're keeping it straightforward and sustainable.

Defining Your Fitness Goals:

To kick things off, let's get clear on what you want to achieve with your minimalist exercise routine. Are you aiming to shed some pounds, build muscle, increase flexibility, get fit for a certain sport or simply boost your overall wellness?

Knowing your goals will serve as your compass throughout this journey.

Choosing Your Workout Style:

Now, think about what kind of workouts resonate with you. Are you a fan of bodyweight exercises that you can do anywhere, anytime? Does the idea of yoga's mind-body connection appeal to you? Perhaps brisk walks in the park for that refreshing cardio, or even some high-intensity interval training (HIIT) to maximize your workout in less time? The choice is yours.

Flexible Workout Times:

Life can get pretty hectic, and we get that. Your exercise routine needs to flex with your schedule. Whether you can spare a quick 15 minutes, a solid 30, or more, the key is consistency & setting a target that you can turn up for every day.

Even if some days it's just 5 minutes to get your heart rate up this will still improve cardiovascular health, boost your mood, increase energy, and enhance fitness by building consistency in a more sustainable and realistic exercise routine.

The key is finding a balance that works for you and aligns with your goals. For some people, daily short workouts fit well into their routine, while others prefer longer, more intense sessions a few times a week.

The most important thing is to choose an exercise routine that you enjoy and can sustain over time, as consistency is the key to reaping the long-term benefits of exercise.

Adding a Dash of Variety:

Keep the fitness flame alive by injecting some variety into your plan. Consider rotating exercises, experimenting with new activities like dancing or trying a new sport. Mixing things up keeps it interesting and helps you discover what you truly enjoy.

It's essential to recognise that different types of exercises bring various benefits to the table.

Cardiovascular workouts like running or cycling elevate your heart rate, enhancing your overall fitness and stamina.

Strength-building exercises, whether through weightlifting or bodyweight training, help you build and maintain lean muscle mass, boosting your metabolism and physical strength.

On the other hand, stretching exercises like yoga or pilates promote flexibility, reduce the risk of injury, and contribute to better posture.

To truly embrace the minimalist approach to exercise, consider adopting a holistic view of fitness. Rather than focusing solely on one aspect, aim for a balanced blend of cardiovascular workouts, strength training, stretching, and even mindful relaxation practices.

Each element plays a unique role in your well-being, ensuring that you stay physically fit, mentally sharp, and emotionally resilient. By incorporating these various dimensions of exercise into your routine, you'll not only achieve a well-rounded fitness level but also discover a deeper connection to your body and mind.

Listening to Your Body:

Your body is your greatest ally on your minimalist exercise journey. It's an intuitive and responsive system that constantly communicates its needs, capabilities, and boundaries.

Tuning in to these signals is key to maintaining a sustainable and enjoyable fitness routine. If at any point during your workouts, something doesn't feel quite right or seems out of sync with your objectives, it's essential to heed these messages.

For instance, if you're pushing yourself too hard during a session, your body may send signals in the form of discomfort, fatigue, or even pain. Instead of pushing through, this is the moment to pause, reassess, and make adjustments.

Maybe you need to lower the intensity, modify the exercise, or simply take a break. By doing so, you honour your body's wisdom, preventing potential injuries and ensuring that your fitness journey remains a positive experience.

Moreover, your body is also an incredible source of feedback and progress tracking. As you engage in your minimalist exercise routine, you'll notice changes – increased endurance, improved flexibility, or enhanced strength.

These transformations serve as tangible evidence of your efforts paying off. Celebrate these milestones, no matter how small they may seem, as they reflect your commitment to a healthier, more vibrant you.

Ultimately, embracing this philosophy of listening to your body fosters a profound connection between your physical self and your overall well-being.

It's a reminder that your fitness journey is uniquely yours, and every step you take should be in harmony with your body's signals, aligning with your goals, and promoting a sustainable and balanced approach to exercise.

By heeding your body's wisdom, you ensure that your minimalist exercise routine becomes a lifelong practice filled with joy, vitality, and wellness.

Your body knows best. If something doesn't feel quite right or doesn't align with your goals, don't hesitate to make adjustments. This journey is about being in tune with yourself.

Seamless Integration into Daily Life:

Remember, minimalism is about enhancing your life, not complicating it. Craft a workout plan that seamlessly fits into your daily routines, so it becomes an integral part of your lifestyle.

Minimalism is all about simplifying, decluttering, and streamlining, and this philosophy extends beautifully into your exercise routine.

The aim is to create a workout plan that becomes as second nature as brushing your teeth or sipping your morning coffee.

This means it doesn't need to be an elaborate or time-consuming affair. Quite the opposite... It should effortlessly blend into your daily life, becoming an integral part of your routine without causing disruptions or added stress.

One way to do this is by selecting exercises that can be seamlessly incorporated into your day-to-day activities.

For example, opting for bodyweight exercises like squats or lunges while you're waiting for your morning coffee to brew or engaging in quick stretching sessions during work breaks can be incredibly effective.

These micro-workouts are designed to be simple, efficient, and can be completed in just a few minutes. By weaving them into your daily life, you'll gradually build strength, flexibility, and fitness without even realising it.

Remember, minimalism is about enhancing your life, not complicating it. Craft a workout plan that seamlessly fits into your daily routines, so it becomes an integral part of your lifestyle.

Celebrating the Wins:

In your minimalist exercise journey, celebrating your progress is crucial. Each step, no matter how small, is a triumph in itself.

Take a moment to acknowledge and appreciate your dedication, discipline, and the positive changes you're making in your life. These small victories are the building blocks of your fitness and well-being, and they deserve recognition.

Sometimes, it's easy to fixate on the end goal, whether it's achieving a specific fitness level, losing weight, or mastering a challenging yoga pose. While having goals is essential, it's equally important to savour the journey and the improvements you notice along the way.

Did you do one more push-up this week than last? Did you find a new sense of calm during your meditation session? These are all signs of progress.

Embrace the idea that this journey is not a race but a lifelong adventure. It's not just about reaching the destination; it's about the experiences, lessons, and growth you encounter along the way.

Enjoy the ride, and remember that every step forward is worth celebrating.

Now, with this roadmap in hand, it's your turn to create a minimalist exercise plan that's tailored to your needs and preferences. The most effective routine is one that you genuinely enjoy and can stick to, so let's craft a plan that suits you perfectly.

Time-Saving Techniques

In our fast-paced world, finding time for exercise can be challenging, but it's far from impossible. With some clever strategies and a touch of creativity, you can make the most of your available time and ensure your fitness journey remains consistent and fulfilling. Here are some time-saving techniques to help you achieve just that:

Maximizing Workout Efficiency:

Life can get busy, and dedicating an hour or more to the gym might not always be feasible. Instead, consider workouts designed for maximum efficiency. High-Intensity Interval Training (HIIT) and circuit workouts are excellent choices for efficient workouts.

These routines are designed to deliver a potent workout in a shorter time frame, making them perfect for individuals with packed schedules. In just 10-30 minutes, you can achieve a challenging and rewarding exercise session.

Incorporating Short, Effective Workouts:

Short, effective workouts can be seamlessly integrated into your daily routine. Think of them as exercise "snacks" that keep your energy levels up throughout the day.

Whether it's a set of bodyweight squats, a few minutes of planking, or a quick yoga flow, these micro-workouts provide a burst of activity without overwhelming your schedule.

Embracing Micro-Workouts:

Micro-workouts are all about quick, targeted exercises that

focus on specific muscle groups. These bite-sized sessions can be sprinkled throughout your day.

For instance, you can perform calf raises while brushing your teeth, do a few lunges while waiting for your coffee to brew, or engage in desk stretches during work breaks i.e. if using short breaks with the Pomodoro technique as discussed in week 7.

These tiny efforts add up, contributing to your overall fitness without requiring a large time commitment.

Stay Active Throughout the Day:

Exercise doesn't have to be confined to formal workouts. Encourage yourself to stay active throughout the day by adopting small lifestyle changes.

Opt for the stairs instead of the elevator, walk or bike to work, or take short breaks to stretch and move around during sedentary tasks.

These continuous bursts of activity keep your body engaged and your mind refreshed, all without the need for structured workouts.

Remember, your fitness journey should enhance your life, not complicate it. These time-saving techniques allow you to weave exercise seamlessly into your daily routine, ensuring that it becomes a sustainable and enjoyable part of your minimalist lifestyle.

Flexibility and Adaptability

In the realm of minimalist exercise, one key principle stands out: flexibility. Your fitness journey should be as adaptable as the minimalist lifestyle itself, allowing you to navigate various life situations with ease. Here's why flexibility is vital and how you can incorporate it into your exercise routine:

Embracing Flexibility:

Life is unpredictable, and your exercise routine should be able to bend and adapt accordingly.

While consistency is valuable, it shouldn't come at the cost of rigid inflexibility.

Recognize that there will be days when your initial workout plans might not align with reality due to unforeseen circumstances or changing priorities.

Adapting to Changing Circumstances:

Whether it's travel, work commitments, or family responsibilities, there will be times when your usual workout environment is disrupted.

Instead of getting discouraged, consider these moments as opportunities to adapt.

You can explore local fitness options when travelling or create a condensed workout plan during a busy work week.

The key is to find ways to stay active and maintain your commitment to fitness, even in challenging situations.

Modifying Exercises:

Everyone's fitness journey is unique, and it's essential to tailor your exercises to your individual needs and limitations.

If you're a beginner, start with exercises that match your fitness level. If you have physical limitations or injuries, seek exercises that accommodate them without exacerbating the issue.

For instance, swimming or water aerobics can be gentle on the joints, while resistance band workouts offer an effective alternative to traditional weightlifting without the need for racks of expensive dumbbells.

Remember, a minimalist exercise routine should empower you to stay active and healthy while adapting to the ever-changing landscape of life. Flexibility is your ally in this journey, allowing you to maintain your commitment to fitness, regardless of what life throws your way.

Accountability and Progress Tracking

In the pursuit of a minimalist exercise routine, accountability and progress tracking serve as your guiding lights, helping you stay on course and celebrate your victories along the way.

Let's delve into why these elements are essential and how to incorporate them into your fitness journey:

The Power of Accountability:

Accountability isn't about strict self-discipline or self-punishment. Instead, it's a supportive tool that keeps you on track and reinforces your commitment.

When you have someone or something to be accountable to, whether it's a workout buddy, coach, or even just yourself, it becomes harder to skip a workout or lose sight of your fitness goals.

Tracking Your Fitness Journey:

Tracking your progress offers undeniable benefits. It allows you to see how far you've come and identifies areas that may need improvement.

There are various methods to monitor your fitness achievements, depending on your preferences. Fitness apps, such as MyFitnessPal or Strava, offer convenient ways to record workouts and measure performance.

Alternatively, a fitness journal can be a simple yet effective tool to note your workouts, track your weight or body measurements, and record how you feel after each session.

Celebrating Milestones:

Celebrating your fitness milestones, whether big or small, is crucial to maintaining motivation and a sense of accomplishment.

Each milestone signifies progress and serves as a reminder of your dedication. Treat yourself when you reach a particular goal—whether it's a relaxing massage or taking time to make a special healthy meal.

These rewards not only celebrate your achievements but also act as motivation for the next phase of your fitness journey.

Accountability and progress tracking are your companions on this minimalist exercise journey. They provide structure and motivation while ensuring you stay focused on your fitness goals.

Whether you prefer high-tech solutions or a traditional pen-and-paper approach, find what works best for you, and use it to celebrate each step forward in your fitness journey.

Conclusion and Actionable Steps

As we conclude this exploration into minimalist exercise, let's recap the fundamental principles that can help you thrive with a minimalist exercise routine:

Streamlined Fitness for Wellness:

Minimalist exercise is all about simplifying your approach to fitness and making it an integral part of your life. By prioritising consistency and simplicity, you can achieve your fitness goals without adding unnecessary complexity to your daily routines.

Defining Your Fitness Goals:

The first step in your minimalist exercise journey is to define clear fitness objectives. Consider what you want to achieve—whether it's improved health, increased strength, reduced stress, or enhanced flexibility. Your goals will serve as your compass, guiding your exercise plan.

Crafting a Personalised Plan:

Armed with your fitness goals, create a minimalist exercise plan that aligns with your needs and lifestyle. Choose exercises that resonate with you, whether it's yoga, bodyweight workouts, or a simple daily walk. Decide on a workout duration that fits your schedule, be it 15 minutes, 30 minutes, or more. Remember, the key is consistency.

Staying In Tune with Your Body:

Pay attention to your body's signals. If something doesn't feel right or align with your goals, don't hesitate to make adjustments. This journey is about being in tune with yourself and adapting your exercise routine as needed.

Now, let's take these principles and put them into action:

1. Define Your Fitness Goals:

Take some time to clearly outline your fitness goals. Do you want to train for a specific sport or activity? What do you want to achieve through your minimalist exercise routine?

Write them down in a journal or on your phone to keep them visible.

2. Craft Your Minimalist Exercise Plan:

Create a simple exercise plan that matches your objectives. Choose exercises that you enjoy and that align with your goals. Set aside specific times in your daily or weekly schedule for your workouts.

3. Get Started:

Begin your minimalist exercise routine by dedicating anything from 10-30 minutes a day to moving your body. Whether it's a short yoga session, a brisk walk, or a set of bodyweight exercises, the key is to start small and build from there.

4. Stay Accountable:

Find a way to stay accountable for your workouts. It could be a workout buddy, an app that tracks your progress, or a simple journal where you record your exercise sessions.

5. Celebrate Your Progress:

As you embark on your minimalist exercise journey, remember to celebrate your small victories along the way. Each step forward is a testament to your commitment and resilience.

Incorporate these actionable steps into your week, and watch as your minimalist exercise routine becomes a natural and enriching part of your daily life.

Whether you're striving for better physical health or seeking mental clarity, your journey to thrive through minimalist exercise starts with a single step.

Week 11: Simplifying Relationships for Deeper Connections

In today's fast-paced and digitally connected world, our personal and professional relationships can become cluttered and overwhelming.

Many of us struggle to maintain meaningful connections with the people in our lives due to various distractions and time constraints.

Simplifying relationships involves consciously choosing to prioritise and invest in the connections that truly matter. This means letting go of toxic relationships, setting healthy boundaries, and focusing on building deeper, more fulfilling connections with the people who bring value to our lives.

Simplifying relationships can have numerous benefits for our mental health, emotional well-being, and overall quality of life.

By focusing on the relationships that matter most, we can cultivate stronger connections and develop a deeper sense of belonging and community. We can also reduce stress and emotional burden by letting go of negative or draining relationships that no longer serve us.

In this weeks chapter, we will explore various techniques and strategies for simplifying relationships and building stronger connections with the people in our lives.

Relationships can have a significant impact on one's mental health and overall well-being. Unhealthy or toxic relationships can lead to stress, anxiety, and even depression.

This is why simplifying relationships is important. Simplifying relationships involves identifying and letting go of unhealthy relationships while focusing on building stronger and more fulfilling connections.

By simplifying relationships, we can reduce stress, improve our mental health, and even create space for new and positive relationships.

Minimalism in relationships can also help individuals to identify and focus on the relationships that truly matter.

By simplifying relationships, individuals can prioritise their time and energy on the relationships that bring them the most joy and fulfilment. This can lead to a deeper sense of connection, more meaningful conversations, and stronger bonds.

Overall, simplifying relationships can lead to a more fulfilling and happy life.

Tips for Simplifying Relationships

When it comes to simplifying relationships, there are a few key tips that can help you streamline your connections and build stronger bonds.

First and foremost, it's important to identify any toxic or unfulfilling relationships in your life and set healthy boundaries to protect yourself. This might mean distancing yourself from certain people or having difficult conversations to address issues that have been causing tension or conflict.

Another important aspect of simplifying relationships is prioritising communication and vulnerability. When we are open and honest with those we care about, we can build deeper and more meaningful connections.

This might mean having more intentional conversations, actively listening to others, and being willing to share your own thoughts and feelings as well. By prioritising communication and vulnerability, you can create a safe and supportive space for yourself and those around you.

As you've worked on various aspects of your well-being over the past weeks, including decluttering, meditation, slowing down, exercising for mental health, and adopting a balanced diet, you've been preparing your mental and emotional state.

These practices can help you feel more confident, clear-minded, and at peace when engaging in difficult or deep conversations. Remember, your journey towards a simpler, more mindful life isn't just about decluttering your physical space; it's also about creating mental space for positive and meaningful interactions with others.

Finally, it's important to focus on quality over quantity when it comes to relationships. Instead of trying to maintain a large network of acquaintances or surface-level connections, prioritise the relationships that truly matter to you.

This might mean investing more time and energy into close friendships or family relationships or cultivating new connections with people who share your values and interests. By focusing on quality over quantity, you can create more meaningful and fulfilling relationships in your life.

Of course, simplifying relationships is often easier said than done. It can be challenging to identify toxic relationships or set healthy boundaries, and it can be difficult to prioritise communication and vulnerability when we're used to keeping our guard up or avoiding difficult conversations.

However, by taking small steps and being intentional about your relationships, you can start to build stronger connections and create a more fulfilling social life.

One way to simplify relationships is to take inventory of your current connections and evaluate which ones are truly adding value to your life. This might mean making a list of the people you spend time with regularly and reflecting on how each relationship makes you feel.

Are there any relationships that leave you feeling drained or unhappy? Are there others that bring you joy and fulfilment? By identifying which relationships are worth investing in and which ones are not, you can start to focus your time and energy on the connections that truly matter.

Another important step in simplifying relationships is learning to set boundaries and communicate your needs effectively. This might mean having difficult conversations with friends or family members about how they treat you or being more intentional about the time you spend with certain people.

By setting clear boundaries and communicating your needs, you can create healthier and more fulfilling relationships that better align with your values and priorities.

Ultimately, simplifying relationships is all about focusing on what truly matters and cultivating deeper connections with those around you. By being intentional about your relationships and prioritising communication, vulnerability, and quality over quantity, you can build stronger bonds and create a more fulfilling social life.

How to Build Stronger Connections by Simplifying Relationships

Building stronger connections through minimalism in relationships involves an intentional effort to simplify and strengthen existing relationships, as well as cultivate new ones that align with one's values and priorities.

Here are some steps to take:

Reflect on your values and priorities:

Consider what is important to you in your relationships. What qualities do you value most in the people you surround yourself with? What kind of support or encouragement do you need from your relationships?

Reflecting on these questions can help you clarify what kind of relationships you want to cultivate.

Identify toxic or unfulfilling relationships:

It's important to recognise relationships that are draining, toxic, or unfulfilling.

This could include relationships that involve constant drama, lack of mutual respect, or unhealthy boundaries. Once you identify these relationships, it's important to set boundaries or consider ending the relationship altogether.

Prioritise communication and vulnerability:

Building stronger connections requires open and honest communication. Be willing to express your needs and listen to the needs of others.

This can involve being vulnerable and sharing your thoughts and feelings, as well as actively listening and being empathetic to others.

Focus on quality over quantity:

Having a large number of relationships doesn't necessarily equate to having stronger connections.

Focus on cultivating relationships that bring value and meaning to your life. Invest time and energy in building deeper connections with a smaller group of people.

Consider the amount of time and energy you invest in your relationships and whether they are reciprocal.

It is important to reflect on how many relationships you can realistically maintain without feeling drained, everyone is different here so evaluate and be honest with yourself.

Practice gratitude and appreciation towards your loved ones:

Take time to express your gratitude for the little things they do for you, whether it is a thoughtful gesture or a kind word. Doing so helps you to focus on the positive aspects of your relationships, leading to greater satisfaction and stronger connections.

Additionally, prioritise quality time with your loved ones by engaging in activities that you both enjoy and that promote meaningful conversations.

By doing so, you can create lasting memories and deepen your relationships.

The benefits of having stronger, simpler relationships are numerous. Simplifying relationships can lead to reduced stress and anxiety, increased feelings of fulfilment and happiness, and a greater sense of support and community.

Building stronger connections can also lead to greater opportunities for personal growth and development, as well as a stronger support system and a more positive outlook on life.

Conclusion and Actionable Steps for Week 11

In conclusion, simplifying relationships is an essential part of achieving a balanced and fulfilling life.

By identifying toxic or unfulfilling relationships, prioritising communication and vulnerability, and focusing on quality over quantity in relationships, you can build stronger, simpler connections that promote overall well-being and reduce stress.

To get started with simplifying your relationships this week, here are 3 actionable steps you can take:

1. Assess and Elevate Relationships:

Begin the week by reflecting on your relationships. Identify those that may be causing stress or negativity, and consider how you can either improve the dynamics or, if necessary, distance yourself. This step is crucial for fostering stronger and more positive connections.

2. Establish Boundaries and Foster Healthy Communication:

Once you've identified areas for improvement, set clear boundaries in your relationships. Prioritise open and healthy communication, even if it means having challenging conversations. By doing so, you create an environment for stronger, more authentic connections.

3. Focus on Quality over Quantity in Relationships:

Shift your focus from maintaining numerous superficial connections to nurturing fewer, but deeper and more meaningful relationships. Invest time and energy in the people who bring positivity and support into your life, fostering a sense of fulfilment, love and connection.

By taking these simple steps, you can begin to simplify your relationships and build stronger connections that promote overall well-being and happiness.

Minimalism isn't about cutting people out of your life entirely, but rather about focusing on what's truly important and cultivating stronger, simpler connections with those that matter the most to you.

Week 12: Living Sustainably Through Minimalism

In today's society, consumption and material possessions are often equated with success and happiness. However, this mindset can have negative consequences for both our mental health and our planets health.

Higher levels of consumption lead to more waste and a greater impact on the environment, contributing to issues such as global warming, pollution, habitat loss, and resource depletion. Additionally, the accumulation of material possessions can lead to clutter, stress, and anxiety.

One way to combat these issues is through a shift towards lower consumption and mindful consumerism. By focusing on buying and using only what we need, we can reduce our waste and overall impact on the environment.

This mindset not only benefits the planet, but it can also improve our mental health by promoting a simpler, more minimalist lifestyle. Instead of constantly striving for more possessions and wealth, we can learn to appreciate what we already have and prioritise experiences and relationships over material goods.

Additionally, a minimalist mindset can also help with the transition towards a low-waste lifestyle. By only buying what is truly necessary and avoiding excessive packaging and single-use items, we can significantly reduce our waste output.

This means being mindful of the products we purchase, including the groceries we buy and the clothes we wear. It involves finding alternatives to disposable items, such as using reusable containers and bags, and choosing durable and long-lasting items over fast fashion.

This not only benefits the environment, but it can also save money and promote a sense of simplicity and contentment with fewer material possessions.

Why Incorporating Minimalism is Important to Living More Sustainably

Living more sustainably is becoming increasingly important as the negative impact of excessive consumption on the environment becomes more apparent.

With limited natural resources and growing concerns about climate change and pollution, it is essential to adopt a more mindful approach to consumption.

Incorporating minimalism into daily life can help reduce waste and minimise our environmental impact.

The overconsumption of goods, such as fast fashion and single-use plastics, has significant consequences on the environment. Manufacturing these products requires vast amounts of energy and resources, contributing to greenhouse gas emissions and pollution.

Furthermore, the disposal of these goods often leads to waste, which can take centuries to decompose and end up polluting our oceans and natural habitats.

By adopting a minimalist mindset and being more mindful about our consumption, we can reduce the demand for these products and minimise our negative impact on the environment.

In addition to the environmental benefits, a minimalist approach to consumption can also lead to a more fulfilling and stress-free lifestyle. By focusing on what is truly important and necessary, we can eliminate clutter and distractions in our lives, allowing us to prioritise our mental and emotional well-being.

By living more slowly, intentionally and simply as discussed in previous weeks, we can experience the benefits of having less physical possessions, and feel a sense of freedom from the constant need to acquire more.

Tips for Incorporating Minimalism to Live More Sustainably

One of the easiest ways to incorporate minimalism into your daily life for a more sustainable lifestyle is by reducing your consumption of single-use products.

Single-use products are designed for one-time use and are often made of plastic or other non-biodegradable materials. These products end up in landfills or oceans, contributing to pollution and environmental degradation.

By choosing reusable alternatives, such as water bottles, cloth bags, and food containers, you can significantly reduce your waste output and overall consumption.

Not only does this benefit the environment, but it can also save you money in the long run by avoiding constant purchases of disposable items.

Focusing on quality over quantity in purchases

Another way to live more sustainably through minimalism is by prioritising quality over quantity in your purchases.

Instead of buying cheap, disposable items, invest in high-quality products that will last longer and reduce the need for constant replacement.

This approach applies to various aspects of life, from clothing and furniture to household appliances and electronics. By choosing quality over quantity, you can not only save money in the long run but also reduce your overall consumption and waste output.

Adopting a circular economy mindset

Lastly, incorporating a circular economy mindset into your daily life can further contribute to a more sustainable lifestyle.

A circular economy is an economic model that prioritises the use of resources and materials in a closed-loop system, reducing waste and maximising efficiency.

By adopting a circular economy mindset, you can implement practices such as composting, upcycling, and recycling, among others, to extend the life of products and reduce their environmental impact.

Additionally, you can also support companies that prioritise sustainability and ethical practices in their production, further contributing to a more sustainable and responsible consumption culture.

By reducing consumption, and waste output, and focusing on quality over quantity, we can create a more sustainable lifestyle that benefits ourselves and future generations.

By adopting a circular economy mindset, we can maximise the

use of resources and contribute to a closed-loop system that minimises waste and environmental impact.

How to Build a Sustainable Minimalist Lifestyle

Living a sustainable minimalist lifestyle involves intentionally reducing as much of our negative environmental footprints as we can, by reducing consumption and waste.

Here are some steps to take in order to build a sustainable minimalist lifestyle:

Assess your current consumption:

Take a look at your current consumption patterns and evaluate what areas you could reduce that would have a positive impact on the planet. The kinds of things that if a lot of people done them would make a big difference.

This could be anything from reducing your meat intake to using a reusable water bottle & filter or buying glass water bottles that are easier to recycle rather than buying plastic bottles.

Are there any shops near to you that focus on zero waste / no packaging that you could start doing some of you shopping at? Are there any veg box schemes that offer more eco-friendly packaging or no packaging where possible?

Anything you do buy with plastic try to make sure it is highly likely to be recycled by researching what the recycling logos on different plastics mean, this will show you how likely these items are to get recycled in your local recycling bins.

Prioritise quality over quantity:

A theme that rings true throughout this book and in minimalism.

When making purchases, focus on buying high-quality items that are built to last rather than cheaper items that will need to be replaced frequently.

This can help reduce waste and save money in the long run.

Practice a circular economy mindset:

Instead of throwing away items that are no longer needed, consider ways to give them a second life.

This could involve donating clothes to a thrift store, repurposing old furniture, selling used items second-hand, or composting food scraps.

The benefits of living a sustainable minimalist lifestyle go beyond just helping the environment.

By consuming less and focusing on quality over quantity, individuals may find that they have more financial freedom and less stress associated with clutter and excess possessions.

Additionally, living a more sustainable lifestyle can provide a sense of purpose and fulfilment as individuals actively work towards reducing their impact on the planet.

Furthermore, by reducing consumption and waste, individuals can also inspire others to follow suit and adopt more sustainable habits. Building a sustainable minimalist lifestyle is a small but important step towards a more sustainable future for all.

Maintaining a Sustainable Minimalist Lifestyle

Once you have established a sustainable minimalist lifestyle, it's important to maintain it for the long term. Here are some tips for staying on track:

Consistency is Key:

Consistency is important when it comes to maintaining a sustainable minimalist lifestyle.

Continue to practice the habits that have worked well for you and stay committed to reducing your waste and consumption.

Check in with yourself at least every few months to see if you have started slipping back into bad habits that aren't so good for the mind or planet and readjust accordingly.

Be Mindful of Your Purchases:

When making purchases, continue to focus on quality over quantity. Make sure that the items you purchase are sustainable and align with your values.

Remember that every purchase you make has an impact on the environment, so choose wisely.

Find Ways to Reduce Waste:

Continue to find ways to reduce your waste by using reusable products and avoiding single-use items as much as possible.

Compost food scraps and recycle. Avoid throwing things into landfills whenever there is a better option to further reduce your environmental impact.

Incorporate Minimalism into Your Habits:

Look at all the habits you have stacked so far in this book and you will see plenty of reasons why living a minimalist lifestyle has a positive impact on the planet.

Daily minimalist habits you can form to benefit the environment can include meal planning to reduce food waste, reducing energy consumption by turning off lights and unplugging electronics when not in use, and choosing sustainable transportation options like walking, biking, or public transportation.

Keep Learning:

Stay informed about the latest sustainability trends and continue to learn about how you can reduce your environmental impact.

Stay curious and open to new ideas and approaches.

By incorporating these tips into your daily life, you can maintain a sustainable minimalist lifestyle and make a positive impact on the environment.

Conclusion and Actionable Steps for Week 12

Incorporating minimalism into your lifestyle can have a significant positive impact on the environment by reducing waste and consumption.

Additionally, it can lead to a more mindful approach to consumption and a more balanced and sustainable lifestyle.

To start living more sustainably through minimalism, try the following minimalist steps in Week 12:

1. Reduce your consumption of single-use products:

Instead opt for reusable alternatives i.e. refillable coffee cups, reusable straws, lunch boxes and shopping bags.

2. Focus on quality over quantity when making purchases:

Whether big or small, always ask yourself if it's a necessary purchase, and make sure the items align with your values and are sustainable.

3. Incorporate minimalism into your daily habits :

Focus on your minimalist habits as discussed previously such as reducing food waste through meal planning or reducing energy consumption by turning off lights and electronics when not in use.

By implementing these steps and maintaining a sustainable minimalist lifestyle, you can make a positive impact on the environment while also leading a more balanced and intentional life.

Conclusion: Your New Mindful Habits for Peace and Clarity

Recap of the 12-Week Minimalism Challenge

In the last 12 weeks, we have explored various aspects of minimalism and stacking a new minimalist habit each week to benefit our lives.

We have begun incorporating good practices week by week such as decluttering, mindful consumption, meditation, digital detox, slow living, mindful eating, and scheduling, and began to improve our financial stability and work-life balance.

We have learned how to simplify our lives, reduce stress and anxiety, and create more time and space for the things that truly matter.

Through this challenge, we have discovered that minimalism is not just about getting rid of physical possessions, but also about letting go of mental and emotional clutter.

We have learned how to cultivate mindfulness, gratitude, and intentional living in our daily lives.

Overall, this 12-week journey has been about creating a life of purpose, meaning, and joy.

We have explored how a mindful approach to minimalism can help us live a more fulfilling life by focusing on what truly matters to us.

Final Thoughts and Actionable Steps Going Forward

As we come to the end of this 12-week journey towards mindful minimalism, it's important to reflect on the progress made and the benefits gained.

By simplifying our lives and decluttering our physical and mental spaces, we've created more room for peace, clarity, and intentionality. We've also gained a greater appreciation for the things that truly matter in life and reduced our reliance on material possessions.

Moving forward, it's important to continue practising mindful minimalism in our daily lives.

This can involve taking small steps to reduce waste and consumption, being mindful of our thoughts and emotions, and prioritising experiences and relationships over material possessions.

CONCLUSION: YOUR NEW MINDFUL HABITS FOR PEACE AND CLARITY

One actionable step towards mindful minimalism is to continue decluttering regularly, just as we started to do from week 1.

By doing so, we can ensure that our physical spaces remain clutter-free and conducive to a peaceful and productive mindset.

This can involve creating a regular tidying + decluttering schedule and setting aside time each week or month to go through our possessions and let go of those that no longer serve us.

Another actionable step is to practice gratitude on a regular basis. By taking the time to appreciate the things we have, we can maintain a mindset of abundance and reduce our tendency to always want more.

This can involve keeping a gratitude journal, practising daily affirmations, or simply taking a few minutes each day to reflect on the good things in our lives.

In conclusion, the benefits of mindful minimalism are numerous and far-reaching, and the journey towards a simpler and more intentional life is a lifelong one.

By continuing to practice mindful minimalism in our daily lives, we can continue to experience the peace, clarity, and intentionality that this lifestyle offers.

If on reflection you notice any of the areas in your life that we have covered in this book start to dwindle, you can always revisit this book and redo that week to start up that positive habit once again.

Let us embrace this journey with open hearts and minds, and continue to grow and evolve towards our best selves.

Thank You for Reading Mindful Minimalism

I hope you've enjoyed and found value in this guide to living a simpler, more meaningful life through minimalism. Your time and commitment to self-improvement is truly appreciated.

I wrote this book with the hope of helping other people who, like me, have trouble organising their lives and finding peace of mind.

If you found this book helpful or inspiring, please consider leaving a review on your favourite platform.

Your feedback helps others discover the benefits of mindful minimalism and guides them on their journey too.

Remember, simplicity is not just about decluttering physical spaces; it's a pathway to greater clarity, fulfilment, and peace.

Keep embracing the minimalist lifestyle, and may it bring you joy and contentment.

With gratitude,

MINIMALISM

Dean Christopher

Printed in Great Britain
by Amazon